THE EXPLOITERS

Who They Are,
What They Do,
and
Why They Do It

Jack Abramoff
Marc Dreier
Enron
Elmry de Hory
Bunker Hunt
Clifford Irving
Bernie Madoff
Michael Milken
Jack Molinas
Richard M. Nixon
Play Misty for Me
Misery
Fatal Attraction
All About Eve

Don Juan

DR. HARVEY A. KAPLAN

Contents

Introduction

Throughout civilization we have witnessed everything from con artists, liars, cheats, frauds and even imposters in this century. To deceive and exploit, to trick with shrewd and clever tactics is surely a basic illness of modern society. In all kinds of exploitation there are elements of fraud or deception.

The exploiter is a particular kind of character type who often does not appear so much different from the average person until you begin to add up and understand the aim of their actions. Relationships always have an ulterior motive and there is a decided lack of integrity and empathy toward those they come into contact. You can never be sure whether their feelings toward you are honest and sincere or rather, that they are putting on some act to win you over.

The exploiter is able to keep up his appearances by attenuating his aggression and applying it to being clever and tricky. In a way they enter more actively into competition with their victim. They lean toward proving their superiority by defeating the other person. Their aim in life is the pursuit of putting something over and this often comes as a result of outright betrayal of trust. Their empathy is minimal and they rarely seem to feel awful when realizing how destructive they have been. Obviously, they are not the kind we ought to ever trust or even get that close to even though they can exude extreme charm and offer multitudes of help. This is all in the quest to exploit and manipulate both the other and the situation.

What we do find in the end is that they are extremely ambitious and when pushed will resort to all kinds of deviances to win the day. In fact, their ambition is fueled by a heightened greed that makes losing not a viable option for them. No, they must win and of course, they must win at all costs. In this pursuit, they often appear like heroes who are energized by godlike powers and energies. The problem is that they cannot contemplate not being the best, the brightest and the most skilled. All of this comes at a terrible price - that being their own destructiveness - they invariably get caught at it and unfortunately the victim pays the price. I hope to highlight in the following chapters an array of exploitative personalities together with their underlying psychological complexities. I hope that this will give the reader a deeper understanding of what motivates these people to do what they feel they must. Lying, deceit, corruptibility is one of the supreme vices in our culture. We must always be on guard for this, otherwise we pay the price of being the exploiter's prey.

I wish to illustrate two kinds of exploiters, one who breaks the law outright and the other who tries to win in a most deceptive way exploiting the very sport she is engaged. .

On 21 April 1980, Rosie Ruiz, a 23-year-old New Yorker, was the first woman to cross the finish line in the Boston Marathon. She had achieved the third fastest time ever recorded for a female runner (two hours, thirty-one minutes, and fifty-six seconds), which was made all the more remarkable by the fact that she looked remarkably sweat-free and relaxed as she climbed the winner's podium to accept her wreath. However, race officials almost immediately began to question her victory.

The problem was that no one could remember having seen her during the race. Monitors at the various race checkpoints hadn't seen her, nor had any of the other runners. Numerous photographs taken during the race failed to contain any sign of her. Her absence was overwhelming. Finally, a few members of the crowd came forward to reveal that they had seen her jump into the race during its final half-mile. Apparently she had then simply sprinted to the finish line.

As race officials prepared to announce her disqualification from the race, they discovered evidence that she had also cheated during the earlier New York marathon, where she had earned the time that had qualified her to run in the Boston marathon. She had apparently achieved her time in New York by riding the subway. Officials stripped her of her Boston victory and awarded the title to the real winner, Jackie Gareau.

In another instance, we have the case of Rajat Gupta, a former Goldman Sachs director who was found guilty of leaking the bank's boardroom discussion to his hedge fund friend. A taped conversation to Raj Rajaratnam a hedge fund manager went like this: "I heard yesterday from somebody who's on the board of Goldman Sachs that they are going to lose $2 per share." At his trial, Mr. Gupta was sentenced to two years in prison. Mr. Gupta who came to this country from South Asia rose to the highest ranks of business. He was once one of the world's most admired executives having served for a decade as the global chairman of the management consultant firm, McKinsey & Company.

The judge in the case recounted damning evidence that phone logs and trading records

indicated that less than one minute after hanging up from a Goldman board call, Mr. Gupta phoned Mr. Rajaratnam who quickly bought about $35 million worth of Goldman stock. This relationship which consisted of passing off insider trading information continued for some time. We might wonder why would a person with the kinds of prestige, achievement and money resort to such criminal activity. Was he trying to cheat the system, put something over on his colleagues or needed to feel the exhilaration of the activity itself. Essentially he exploited the very economic system that brought him his success. And the puzzling question is why resort to such activity? I will try to answer these questions in the cases that follow.

Chapter One

High School Reunion
Two Friends

Tom Jacobs and Jack Roth had been friends since elementary school. They grew up within blocks of each other in the outer reaches of the Bronx, playing sports and socializing often. At their public elementary school, Tom and Jack were in the same class. In high school, different classes and schedules separated them on weekdays, but after school and on weekends they remained almost inseparable—like brothers—and a strong bond existed between them.

Their teachers evaluated both boys as bright, ambitious, and driven to succeed. Often Tom and Jack would talk for hours on end, sharing their hopes for the future. Tom aspired to go into finance. Jack had a passion for computers. They both dreamed that one day they would conquer the world. Their dreams of the future were exciting and enchanting.

After graduating from high school, the young men attended different colleges, and at the same time their parents moved to different neighborhoods that further separated them. Still Tom and Jack stayed friends and shared their college breaks and summers together as much as they could. After college, however, they drifted apart. They attended each other's weddings, but after that they forged their different careers, and when they started their own families they lost touch completely. They probably would attribute this to the differences in their wives, who were quite different in style and character. In addition, Jack remained in the city while Tom moved to the suburbs.

***

Fifteen years passed. One day Tom and Jack received invitations to their twentieth class high school reunion. At first they both put their invitations aside, having little interest in attending an event representing a former life that seemed light-years in the past. And of course, there was a feeling of awkwardness of revisiting certain experiences they just as well wanted to forget as well as the fear of wondering how they stacked up against their fellow graduates. However, the underlying feeling of missing out on something even unknown to them got both men to reconsider.

The reunion committee chose a hotel close to Manhattan's Penn Station. Jack lived within walking distance of the hotel, and Tom, who now lived in Westchester, could easily attend by taking the same train that he took to work every day. This certainly ruled out one reservation, which was travel. So after much consideration and with significant encouragement from their wives, both men accepted the invitation. In the end they each decided to go, probably because they didn't want to feel as if they would miss out on this event.

Entering the large banquet room where the reunion was held, Tom and Jack spotted each other immediately. The sense of warmth and friendship they felt for each other all those past years was instantly reignited. Oblivious at first to their other classmates, Tom and Jack sat down and eagerly began to catch each other up on their lives. An infectious humor pervaded their conversation. It was as if no time had elapsed; they got caught up in their childhood all over again.

Tom, the more ebullient of the two, proudly touted his successes on Wall Street, his two children, his lovely wife, and the myriad prestigious organizations to which he belonged. Jack, more subdued, told Tom about his life: the large middle-class housing complex on the East Side in which he and his family live and his solid career as a computer programmer in a large firm where he is well respected and earns a good living. It was clear that Jack was not—and had no desire to be—as driven and ambitious as his friend. Security and safety were his goals. Jack mentioned a number of times the importance of having cemented his position at his firm. Jack's goal was to be free of job-related anxiety so that he could devote time to his wife and children and his hobbies while avoiding the stress of uncertainty.

Tom was clearly more of a risk-taker. He had changed companies a number of times in the last fifteen years, each time securing a better paying and more prestigious position. While speaking of his dream to start his own fund and how fervently he wanted to achieve it, Tom's manner grew more intense. Jack was impressed by his friend's passion but also a bit turned off by what he perceived as Tom's boastful, even self-aggrandizing manner. At certain points in their conversation Jack wondered whether Tom was actually talking to him or just using him as a sounding board.

After the old friends had clearly gone over the salient facts of their lives, the conversation took a more congenial turn as they discussed sports, politics, and family vacations. They seemed to welcome the interruption that came when the principal called everyone to take their seats at their assigned tables. This also gave them the opportunity to socialize with some of their classmates.

The current principal of the school took the stage and presented plaques to the highest-achieving alumni and delivered a rousing speech about how the school was progressing. He got a big laugh when he ended his speech by saying, "And guys the school is now co-ed, so look what you missed out on!" From then on there was more of a friendly mixture among the former students. Maybe being an all-boys school had something to do with it, but the friendship and joviality that everyone had hoped for somehow did not come over that way. There were too many guys who weren't there; they had moved to other states and decided not to take the trip back to New York. As the evening drew to a close, Tom and Jack assured each other that they would meet again soon and parted ways with a wealth of warm feeling.

As Jack strolled toward his apartment, his thoughts were filled with Tom. Jack was impressed by Tom's rapid ascent and by his ambition. There was an intensity about him, a strong desire to plough forward, to excel, to impress. But at the same time Jack felt a bit threatened by Tom, and his success made Jack doubt himself. Maybe he should have gone further and faster in life, he thought. In the end Jack wondered whether they really would get together. The impression he took away from the reunion was positive; he would have been sorry to have missed it. Everyone seemed genuinely happy to see him. Getting along with others had always been a priority for him, but he knew that about himself.

On the train ride home to Chappaqua, Tom stared out of the window sporting a huge smile on his face. The evening had brought him much pleasure. Career-wise, Tom felt he compared favorably with most of his old schoolmates. In fact, he knew that he was doing better than most. Some classmates he had looked up to at school were not so impressive as he had remembered. Others he saw as losers who had never gotten anywhere, and of course, a few really excelled. Those were the ones in science and math.

Tom's thoughts then turned to his old buddy Jack. He thought that Jack had been a bit reserved, almost defensive, in his description of himself. Tom couldn't help but feel that Jack didn't want very much for himself. His life seemed circumscribed by rigid, self-imposed boundaries. Granted, Jack had constructed a happy life—he was moderately successful and cared a great deal for his family. But somehow he held himself back. *Hey man, go for it*, Tom had felt like saying to him more than once during the evening. Tom, too, wondered if they would really get together as they had planned.

The next week Jack was sitting at his desk going over some reports when the phone rang. When he picked it up, he was surprised and pleased to hear Tom's voice on the other end of the line.

"Hey buddy, it was really grand seeing you at the reunion. Why don't we follow up on it? I have a window for lunch this Thursday. How about it?"

A creature of habit, Jack did not like going out for lunch but realized that it would seem rigid, if not unfriendly, of him to decline.

"Sounds good to me," said Jack said. "I am really happy that you called."

On Thursday at 1:00 p.m. Tom and Jack found themselves at the Delight Coffee Shop deep in conversation. Tom was telling Jack about a business he had developed the past year. He was running a hedge fund that was starting to bring in some high percentages. Then, abruptly, Tom changed the subject, picking up a conversational thread from their reunion.

"What was that college you went to again?"

"You know I was always interested in everything mechanical, and I was so delighted to get accepted in Rensselaer Poly Tech, where I studied engineering," Jack answered. "It was a good school although a bit isolated where it was located."

"Yes, Troy is in the boondocks," Tom said with a smile. "Math was never one of my favorite subjects, although I did have a knack for business. I was off to Cornell. I enjoyed myself, and it was really a good school. I wished they had a better basketball team, but you can't have everything.

"So dude," Tom continued, "what exactly do you do?"

"As I said, I am a computer programmer," Jack said. "I work out different programs and create customized software for corporations that hire us."

They talked some more then got the check. Tom held up his hand, picked up the check, and said briskly with a smile, "This one is on me." They then went their separate ways, promising they would get together again soon.

As Jack walked back to his office, he went over the lunch in his mind. Tom seemed to provide a new dimension to his life. Jack felt he needed Tom to break down the wall that he had built around himself—a wall that cut him off from a world of possibilities. He saw Tom as a high roller but one who played within the rules of the game. It never crossed his mind that Tom was not a straight shooter.

At their next luncheon, Tom was more focused on his work.

"I found that I can beat the market by almost five percentage points. And it is a safe, non-risk strategy for borrowing money and then lending it out as mortgages to companies that can't get them through the usual sources. Also, my company is building upscale homes in the Hamptons where there is a scarcity of space. I am really excited about the whole deal, and I've got some great people working for me—a few of the guys I've known since college, and they are loyal and hardworking. And you, what's going on?"

"Well," Jack replied, "I usually put my money in conservative investments even though there's a low return. I figure with two kids who eventually will go to college I had better play it real safe. Not that I am always satisfied with the way I do things, but I've seen too many guys get burned, and that's not for me. But your thing really sounds exciting."

This time Jack picked up the check.

As they were leaving the coffee shop Tom turned to Jack. "Hey, next Sunday we are having some people up to our house for a barbecue, and we would love to have you and your family join us. You could see how the other half live." He said the last sentence with a wide grin.

"I'll run it by my wife, but it sounds terrific," Jack said, wryly adding, "And I know we would love to see how the other half live."

Jack's wife, Nancy, was more than happy to visit Tom; it was a chance to go to the country. She had a vague picture in her mind of Tom's wife, who she had not seen in some time.

On Sunday Tom picked up Jack and his family at the Chappaqua train station and drove them to his house. It was a rather grand house: swimming pool, beautiful lawn, a bit ostentatious and opulent. It seemed as if every detail had been planned with much care. Tom introduced them to his family and then started telling Nancy how far he and Jack went back together. Of course Nancy knew all of the details, but Tom seemed to have a need to recount them as a way of making a connection with her.

It was a wonderful day for Jack. His two boys happily played with Jack's kids, and the wives seemed to get along well. During their visit Jack also met a number of Tom's friends, who were all really good guys. They were warm with a spirited sense of humor, and they had a wide range of interests. They were the kinds of guys that Jack would have loved to associate with. At around six o'clock, as previously planned, Tom drove Jack and his family back to the train station and saw them off. Reflecting on their day together, Jack felt as if Tom had really orchestrated a full afternoon.

On the train ride back to the city, Jack told Nancy how wonderful he thought Tom had been—very generous and giving.

"The only reservation I have is that after seeing this huge house they live in, I wonder if I should feel a bit embarrassed with the way we live?" Jack said. "Not that I am unhappy with our lives," he added hastily, seeing Nancy's concerned expression, "but when I see how he has succeeded, I kind of wonder about myself—wonder if I stack up to him and even to his friends."

After thinking a bit, Nancy responded. "You know, darling, just because you and Jack have different goals and lifestyles, that doesn't make our lives any better or worse than his. We never wanted to live in the suburbs, and while our building isn't The Plaza, we have a spacious, comfortable apartment. There's no need for you to compare yourself to Tom—you're two very different people."

"You're right, of course," said Jack a bit sheepishly. "I'm a damn lucky guy, and you're right; his life isn't my thing. I want to be friends with him. I just have to get comfortable with the differences that I see between us."

Over the next few months, Tom and Jack met a few more times for lunch. One time Jack visited Tom at his office and was impressed by the luxurious decor, the expensive paintings by well-known artists, and the panoramic view of the city. Tom looked right at home in his sharp, custom-made suit that fell just right on his trim frame. The Hermès ties and the expensive brightly colored shirts all proclaimed a man who had achieved considerable success and wanted the world to recognize it.

At Tom's office, over a tumbler of aged whiskey, Tom filled Jack in on the particulars of his investing strategy and the profits he was accruing. When Jack left he felt elated—and slightly tipsy—and he felt so good about himself, about knowing a high roller like Tom. Any doubts he may have had about his pal's lifestyle had vanished. *This guy really is infectious in the best way*, Jack thought. In the relatively short time since they had reconnected, Jack had begun to feel better about himself—more open to the world and more optimistic about his life. It was like a whole new story of his life began to emerge and a fantasy about himself that he had repressed over the years now revealed itself to him.

The next time they met Jack said that he would like to put some of his savings in Tom's care—half of his savings, in fact. Tom asked Jack whether he was ready to take such a big plunge, but Jack reassured him that he had talked it over with Nancy and that they had both agreed that he shouldn't be so damn careful about everything.

So Jack invested with Tom, and their relationship continued on a solid path. They socialized often, and after a time Jack even worked up the nerve to invite Tom and his wife, Ellen, to his apartment for dinner. As it turned out, Jack's fears that Tom would look down on his relatively humble flat proved groundless. Tom looked around and pronounced himself impressed.

"This kind of space in Manhattan is fabulous: you walk to work in addition to walking everywhere. You're one lucky guy," Tom said to Jack. Turning to his Ellen he went on. "You know, we should really move to the city and get a place like this, especially when the kids are grown. I have never really been comfortable with that commute."

Jack and Nancy beamed with pleasure.

***

Five years passed. In the summer of 2007, two mammoth hedge funds run by Bear Stearns based on mortgage-backed securities unexpectedly crashed, signaling the beginning of the end of the stock market boom. Tom reassured Jack that his money was safe and that his investments were not subject to market fluctuations.

In September 2008 the US stock market crashed, triggering meltdowns in major markets worldwide. In December the Bernie Madoff scandal broke when the financier admitted that his wealth management business had in effect been a Ponzi scheme. Thousands of his investors—many of them non-profit charities—lost all the money they had invested with him, which was more than $7 billion. Tom sent out a letter to all his investors reassuring them how well structured his company was and that their monthly reports represented real earnings. But five months later a strange and eerie thing happened: Jack called Tom's office and no one answered the phone. He called Tom's house, and again there was no answer.

Perplexed, Jack walked over to Tom's office the next day. When he got there, he saw an eviction notice posted on the glass door. That evening he again called Tom's home. The mechanical voice on the answering machine said that there was no more room for messages. He called Tom's cell phone but to no avail.

His anxiety continued to mount; Jack waited a few days and went over to Tom's office again. This time, through the glass doors, he spotted a few people talking. Jack pounded on the door and kept pounding until one person turned and opened the door.

"What's going on here?" Jack asked. "Is everything all right?"

The person, who introduced himself as Ed Smith, a lawyer, invited him into one of the rooms.

"Look, I want to tell you that things will not be so good for a while," Smith said. "How well do you know Tom?"

"Pretty well. We've been friends since grade school."

"Let me get to the point. Your friend has committed fraud. He took a loan from a bank and misrepresented the particulars of the loan. In fact, he even lied about the address where the loan would be going. We don't think it's all that serious, but all of the investments have been frozen for a while. That's the way the banks operate, nothing unusual." Seeing the dismayed expression on Jack's face he added, "But we feel that things will be on track in a few months. So don't worry."

"But why doesn't he answer the phones if that's the case?"

"I guess his lawyer advised him to keep quiet," Smith said. "It's really all in the hands of the attorneys at this point, but I believe that will clear up soon when we get to the bottom of it all."

With that Jack was led out of the offices. He did feel a bit better but was perplexed about Tom's motives. He couldn't have been that stupid to lie to a bank, or could he, he thought.

In the months that followed, matters got worse, not better. Tom was being charged with all kinds of fraudulent activities. Investigators discovered that Tom had used the hedge fund as if it was an open cash register from which he grabbed money whenever he needed to cover expenses. When the news broke that the CFO of Tom's hedge fund tried to kill himself by throwing himself in front of a train, Jack truly started to panic.

When he could control his anxiety no longer, Jack visited Tom's office again and pounded on the doors until someone came out of one of the rooms. He recognized the man who opened the door as Larry, who he had met at Tom's house in Chappaqua a number of times.

"I remember you from Tom's place," Larry said. "Why don't you come in and we will talk a bit. I can see the worry on your face."

Jack followed Larry into one of the offices and sat opposite him. Larry started the conversation.

"Tom and I were roommates in college. He recruited me after he had started the fund and offered me a great compensation package. I must tell you that this has become a fiasco. One of the principals in the firm broke up his marriage when his wife threw him out of the house for putting their lives and money at risk. And he has two kids. That CFO who threw himself in front of the train didn't kill himself, but he lost an arm. Let me put it to you straight: I think Tom is an out-and-out crook and thief. He lied about everything. We are finding discrepancies in the records that are shocking. He just dipped in and took monies out whenever he felt like it."

Jack shook his head. "You know, I started to get frightened when he kept expanding his lifestyle. First there was the house in the Hamptons. Then he bought the place in Palm Beach and flew down every weekend. Then with the cars—I just began to worry about his spending."

"Well, you should have," Larry responded. "Everyone figured that he was making a lot of money so why not spend it, but some of the charges are frightening. Look, I wish I could talk to you further, but I have a meeting to get to. Don't think all the money is gone, because it isn't. The bank where he committed this fraudulent loan has frozen our money until they get their money back. I think after that things may get better. How much better they get is still not clear, though. So be well, try not to worry too much, and we will be sending out reports to the investors soon."

Jack walked out of the office in a daze. His first thoughts focused on his children's college fund. He was working and his wife had started a job recently so that they had money for living expenses, but almost all his retirement money was sunk into Tom's hedge fund.

How well did I ever really know this guy, Jack thought. Was it all a deceit? Was our whole relationship just one big sham? How could he do this to so many people who he knew for so long? I guess I really didn't know him at all, with all his charm. Could it all have been an act? And how the hell am I going to tell my wife?

When Jack walked into his apartment that evening, Nancy was waiting. "What did you find out?" He told her as much of the story as he could. She waited for him to finish and then looked him in the eye.

"You know you put our family in jeopardy," she said. "I don't know how you could have been taken in this way. Deep down, I never trusted him. So full of himself, and now what? I just hope we can resolve this between us, because the way I feel now is that I am just so angry that you didn't protect us."

Jack didn't know what to say. What have I done? he thought. I only wanted to make more money. What was so wrong with that? Why would I not have trusted him? And what does all of this say about me?

The Mind of the Exploiter

Tom fits the profile of an exploiter, someone who, underneath his considerable charm and apparent savvy, is basically a garden-variety con artist, albeit on a grand scale. Such people often make others suffer while they themselves seem free from the pangs of conscience that guide most people's actions. The exploiter, with his knack for impressing people, with his importance and success, makes his victims feel special and important when he bestows his friendship on them. He unerringly appraises and leverages the vulnerabilities of his prey. Lacking any feelings of remorse, he feels free to exploit the friendships he cultivates, heedless of the havoc and misery he leaves in his wake.

We place a high premium on clever people who have the boldness to put their ideas into action and to succeed in our competitive world. We assume, however, that the ethical constraints that we live by attach to them as well. Our values and the laws that are in place enforce certain restraints on the exercise of cleverness. People must not cheat, lie, or hurt others. They are not supposed to take unfair advantage of another person's trust, nor must they operate outside the constraints of the law.

To exploit means to behave dishonorably for one's own satisfaction or gain. The exploiter does not operate only in the business world. We all know of instances in families or between friends of the flagrant and often systematic exploitation of a hapless victim. We see evidence of this in everyday life. Even in small matters. Consider going to a restaurant with a friend. The bill comes and you both decide to split the bill. You take out a credit card, and your friend says that he wants to pay in cash. But when he gives you money, you realize immediately that the friend has given you less than what the whole bill and the tip would amount to. You let it go and when the waiter brings back the credit card receipt, you write in the tip, knowing you are paying more than your rightful share. You reason to yourself that it is an insignificant matter hardly worth comment. But if this occurs with some regularity, you start to question what your friend is up to. But let's go further: On further examination you find that your friend does this in almost any situation that he encounters. At this point you are dealing with a particular kind of character—someone who seems compelled to gain some advantage in all spheres of his life, yet he has broken no law.

At one time or another we have all behaved in an exploitative manner. We have lied or misrepresented ourselves to achieve our aims— cheating on a test, for example. But for most of us, that mode of behavior is the exception, not the rule, in our lives. It is not an integral part of our character.

But for some a line or boundary of permissible behavior is crossed. Tom, for instance, may not have started out as a con artist. His ability to manipulate others, making them feel as if he always has their best interests at heart, is a talent possessed by many legitimate businessmen. But at some point Tom became so consumed with attaining a winning position in life that he resorted to fraud.

In an article in *The New York Times*, the story evolves in the following manner. Edward Juarez-Pagliocco built a reputation as a national expert on immigrant affairs. An immigrant himself, the man's work earned him keys to cities in Florida and New Jersey. He had a radio show in New York, and he wrote a column for immigrants published in Spanish-language newspapers.

But Juarez-Pagliocco was not who he claimed to be. The companies that he started employed people who falsely alleged to be lawyers and who often made things worse for the immigrants they promised to help, in addition to overcharging for bogus services. These businesses made millions of dollars by exploiting the dreams of New York's immigrant community.

Juarez-Pagliocco used his companies' money to support a lavish lifestyle: paying hefty rent for a luxury apartment in Manhattan and buying a house in New Jersey and a deluxe car. He traveled and ate at posh restaurants on the companies' dime, not to mention making tens of thousands of dollars of withdrawals with his ATM card.

Juarez-Pagliocco's companies advertised widely, and immigrants came to them for services such as obtaining citizenship or a green card. In one case a man seeking a green card paid the organizations more than $18,000 but never received it because of the groups' delays and negligence. That man and other clients faced deportation because of inadequate representation.

We may shake our heads and ask, how could someone so blithely betray the trust of people who believed in him? They knew full well that they were in a position to destroy the lives of others. But far from feeling shame, such people are often excited not only by the lush lifestyle made possible by their deceit but by the skill they possess that enables them to successfully fleece the people who they see as suckers who are foolish enough to trust them. The profit motive becomes almost beside the point; the sense of superiority and power they derive from their misdeeds becomes the dominant motive for their actions.

Deception is the chief tool of the exploiter. Lying, too, is involved, but there is a difference between the two: Lying is the expression of an untruth with the intent to deceive. Deception is the deliberate fabrication or withholding of information that would not allow a person to make a decision in his or her best self-interest. We all lie. For example, if we want to cut short a meeting with a long-winded client, we may say, "It has been very nice having this talk with you." The statement itself is not true, but neither is it an attempt to deceive. It is a social convention. A college professor of mine once related an amusing anecdote: "At Yale," he said, "when you're no longer interested in talking to someone, you say, 'We must have lunch together sometime.' That's what's known at the Yale Good-bye!"

But the serious or heinous lie is meant to aggrandize one's personality. The objective is to present a distorted picture of ourselves rather than be authentic.

In future chapters, I will refer to people who both bend and break the rules in their attempts to exploit others. Their behavior has become unhitched from the moral code that we hope guides our lives.

In sports, specifically in baseball and track and field, the use of prohibited steroids gives athletes an unfair advantage over their competitors. Marion Jones, one of the greatest runners of all time, allegedly resorted to this. The same goes for Barry Bonds, whose prodigious home run output has been attributed to steroids.

In the financial world, Bernard Madoff exploited everyone with whom he came into contact, including close friends and family—and even his mistress. He took their money willingly, knowing full well that he was running a huge Ponzi scheme.

In the political sphere, John Edwards, a former senator from North Carolina and presidential hopeful, ran into trouble when it was revealed that he was having an affair with a writer and fathered a child with her. When confronted about it, he arranged for an employee of his to claim paternity.

Bunker Hunt attempted to corner the silver market in the 1980s. His plan hinged on massive deceptions designed to conceal the amount of silver he owned. In the end, the plan went haywire but not before he drove the price of silver to unheard-of prices. He was fined hundreds of millions of dollars.

Lobbyist Jack Abramoff bilked an Indian tribe out of millions of dollars by promising them that he could secure gambling rights.

In the 1950s, Jack Molinas, a potentially great basketball player, got other players to throw their games so he could place secure bets. The resulting scandal almost destroyed professional basketball. The irony is that he could have made a fine living by dint of his natural talent. His exploitative behavior was tantamount to a compulsion.

The sad part of it all is that the exploiter has no real interest in the other person, save for how he or she can be used in the pursuit of the exploiter's own needs. The other person is devalued and often seen as an object of contempt, a disposable item to be used and discarded or to be kept around for convenience and pleasure. The exploiter derives pleasure from the success of the interaction and experiences a sense of power and exhilaration.

It is important to understand the dynamics underlying the exploiter's actions. It may be an unconscious strategy used to repair some early trauma suffered at the hands of a sibling, parent, or authority figure. The injury, be it emotional or physical, creates feelings of shame and aggression toward the perceived villain. As an adult, the exploiter projects that anger onto others as a way of getting back at the earlier person. There is a restoration of pride and a sense of exhilaration in that a piece of vengeance has been extracted.

These people are more interested in illusion and public image than in living an honest life. They gain esteem through appearances. Once this part of their character becomes tarnished, they become threatened and will do anything to preserve their inflated persona. They don't seem to be embarrassed if they are caught in a lie. They become apologetic and remorseful, making up stories as to why they were forced to do what they did.

Ezra Merkin was a hedge fund manager who funneled $2.4 billion to Wall Street swindler Bernard Madoff without telling his clients where their money was going. His clients thought that Merkin had developed a sophisticated investment strategy when in fact he was simply a middleman. It was not until after Madoff's arrest that Merkin sent a brief note to his clients informing them that their money was probably gone forever. He duped individual investors, non-profits, and charities into believing he was responsible for managing their investments when in actuality he was dumping them into history's largest Ponzi scheme. To add insult to injury, he charged his clients a cumulative $470 million in management fees.

Merkin was a respected member of his community and one who inspired trust. He was the president of his synagogue and maintained a glamorous lifestyle, residing in an $11 million eighteen-room duplex that contained art by famed painters worth an estimated $150 million. Of course, illegally dipping into his company's funds financed this lifestyle.

The Predator-Prey Relationship

Hopefully, we enter into relationships to give and receive gratifications such as friendship, love, support, and appreciation from the other. We represent ourselves to our loved ones, friends, and business associates with honesty and integrity. Relationships that are founded on these principles remain strong and viable.

Exploiters do not enter into relationships with the same wishes or concerns. Their behavior seems to more closely relate to primitive animalistic drives. They become predators who feed off of their prey. They do not stalk and attack their prey for food—their prey provides money, sex, and fame.

The animal hunting its prey is driven by hunger, not animosity. The cat doesn't hate the mouse. If anything, it would be more natural to assume that the mouse hates the cat.

The role of aggression in the animal world and in the evolution of species has been the subject of a large body of literature. Konrad Lorenz defines it as "an instinct like any other in natural conditions...helps to ensure the survival of the individual and the species." Aggression is part of the animal kingdom's basic structure. One species preys and lives upon another as they compete, fight, and victimize others of their kind. "The majority of vertebrates do so...man included," says Lorenz. We ourselves live to an enormous extent upon the lower forms. "Man, as a carnivorous animal, must kill in order to live," notes Lorenz.

Aggression serves several purposes. Every animal must have a minimum of living space and must drive competitors from its territory. There is aggression among males in competing for females, and the latter must be aggressive in protecting their young. Aggression is an essential part of the survival instinct. In fact, aggression predates the concepts of friendship and love by millions of years.

In this sense, the exploiter is a kind of evolutionary throwback. His aggression is different from those who are mad at the world and strike out indiscriminately. Exploitative aggression, rather, is more cold-blooded much like the hunter in seeking his prey for food. In this respect, the exploiter is acting as the predator and aggression of this kind represents one of the universals of the natural order.

Man is both meat-eating (carnivorous) and vegetarian (omnivorous) and therefore takes over traits of the carnivore and the vegetarian. So he inherits a predatory role toward attacking and devouring a weaker prey as a carnivore, and he inherits the aggression of the vegetarian as an omnivore who fights for other reasons such as territory or sexual rivalry. We must remember that animals that are vegetarian do not attack other animals for food but fight for territorial rights. Once man feels that he wants more and more from life and has the faculty to produce and conserve more than the bare and immediate necessities of life, exploitation may follow, leading to feuds, revolutions, and wars—behaviors unknown to the animal world.

The dependence of human young upon the parent lasts much longer than any other species, and the dependence of the adult on his fellows for sustenance is also much greater. Aggressive behavior aimed at advancement is closely bound up with love, hatred, and feelings of frustration toward our fellow humans. It creates all kinds of strife and conflict. This evolves because of our long dependence on the parent who could turn into a frustrating, even hated, object.

Exploiters search their environment to find their prey, and once found they put into play an array of underhanded talents. They charm, seduce, deceive, and lie all in the name of achieving their ends.

Exploiters who stay within the confines of the law have better impulse control and have the capacity for active, consistent work in areas, which permits them partially to fulfill their ambitions and to obtain admiration from others. They have a functioning conscience that provides a check on their impulsivity. However, their stronger-than-usual desire to reach their goals often makes for conflicted personal and professional relationships. We see this with aggressive entrepreneurs who fight against the very people who were their friends just a day or two before.

But under stress and more intensive ambition, some break laws, lie, and cheat if they have to. Their identities become brittle, and they are less able to form a cohesive sense of reality. At that point all bets are off.

We are all susceptible to such types, so it behooves us to be on a continual lookout for the exploiter who could be the predator next door.

This was the story of Jack and Tom. Maybe if the market had not tanked Tom would not have resorted to illegal and unethical actions. What did he feel toward the people who invested with him? Did he see them as suckers whose inferior intelligence made them legitimate marks, or did his compulsion to be better and more successful than his peers override all other considerations?

Ironically, it is probably Tom who is least able to answer these questions as his perception of himself had become hopelessly distorted. Whatever his reasons it is the result that matters. In the end his exploiter pathology led Tom to destroy the lives of those who admired and trusted him. His initial intent may not have been laden with potentially corrupt motives. Yet it seems that once reality became fraught with obstructions he showed his true colors. It is under pressure and stress that often the best of our character emerges, while in others the worst parts rise to the top, much like cream in coffee.

Chapter Two

It's a Jungle Out There
Marc Dreier

A jungle makes us both think and feel about a place that can be both frightening and ferocious. Predatory animals stalk their prey, and only the strongest and smartest survive, while the weak are picked off and devoured as a matter of course. Although passionless in their pursuit, jungle inhabitants spend much of their time devising ways to attack and destroy their victims. The lions have to eat their meat in order to survive. It's nothing personal; that's just the way things are. It's the law of the jungle. Over time particular rules of behavior develop that stabilize the environment, and, therefore, living there may not end up as being that frightening.

In a similar sense, there are predators that roam our paved streets—except that they pose a greater hazard—and they are not as easily recognized as your average lion, tiger, or bear. They dress and act like us—and, even more perilously, we often count them as our friends, colleagues, or even mentors.

Human law and morality has certainly evolved since man has left the jungle millions of years ago. But alas, exploiters still inhabit a jungle, albeit an imaginary one that they've mentally constructed. All ethical considerations fade when they become the stalkers. Nothing stands in their way: they are not guided by laws, written or unwritten, or moral imperatives, or even loyalties. In a perfect world, exploiter-predators would wear a placard around their necks with the words "BEWARE" or

"WATCH OUT" written in large letters for all to see in order for us to protect ourselves.

Unfortunately, like all effective predators, exploiters do not send out warning signals that they are coming to attack, if not intending to wreak havoc. We get to understand who they really are and what they intend to do only after we are left to pick up the pieces in the wake of the devastation they have created.

Such a man was Marc Dreier, whose recklessness knew no bounds and who created such havoc and destroyed so many lives. Now, thankfully, he is safely behind bars.

But first, let's explore a bit of history of the human jungle.

It is a mistake, and one many of us make daily, when we believe that each of us constructs a similar world that we see before us and then choose to live in. Some of us, whether as a function of nature or nurture, are depressive and see the world as having limited opportunities—a sad world—while others perceive themselves as having been deprived and in turn construct a world that is unforgiving and rejecting. Alternatively, some see the world as full of magical possibilities, while still others construct a world full of adventure and excitement. And still others view their lives as being blocked and constricted, and, as it has been said, they believe they have been given the short end of the stick. Marriages often run into trouble when two people with widely divergent world views decide to merge their lives together. They then tend to view the other with a distorted lens.

In this vein the exploiter inhabits and constructs a very particular kind of world. He or she experiences life and work as a jungle, a place where the winners have the capability to destroy the losers or the weaker. Exploiters tend to view their peers in terms of accomplices or enemies. The middle ground fades away for them.

Michael Maccoby, a psychoanalyst and anthropologist who studied issues pertaining to leadership, has identified two types of leaders among others, who he calls lions and foxes (Maccoby 1976). Foxes achieve their ends by use of seduction, manipulation, and betrayal. They are cunning and secretive, with strong narcissistic and sadistic-authoritarian tendencies. Lions, alternatively, dominate through their superior ideas, courage, and strength. Others follow them because of the kind of fear and reverence they inspire. Lions have an almost pathological need to be admired as superior beings. However, foxes and lions share similar characteristics. Both have grandiose ideas. Both are secretive and conspiratorial. They tend to strike out on their own. Even in their home life they seem to control their wives and compete with their children.

In *Social Character in a Mexican Village,* co-authored by Erich Fromm and Michael Maccoby, the two studied industrialization and its effect on peasants from 1920 to 1970. Maccoby and Fromm observed that those in the village who were quickest to break with long-held traditions like fiestas and other customs, believing that the money was better spent on constructing roads or schools, were also quickest to adapt to the capitalistic model—for instance, buying tractors and renting them out to farmers. There were some who were more unique in their strivings. The most successful used even physical force or blackmail and bribes to gain wealth and political influence. They ruthlessly suppressed their opponents and dominated their subordinates.

So while these ambitious villagers supported positive change and development, they also exhibited character traits that caused dissention within the community. They wound up dominating the village economically, politically, culturally, and ideologically. Additionally, they distrusted the people they controlled and feared revenge from those whose land they had gobbled up. They had few friends, only accomplices and servants. While they talked of progress, they were uninterested in the welfare of the poor, condemning the landless day laborers they exploited as lazy and stupid. Most of these men had destructive effects on their wives, children, and others in the village. In short they exploited everyone and everything with which they came into contract.

Of course not all of these hard-nosed personalities are exploiters. What they did led to progress of a certain kind. There were many who made the transition from communal living to capitalism without becoming exploiters. They didn't break laws, practice deceit, or engage in fraud. Many of these kinds of successful men and women rise to the top without manipulating others. Many successes are achieved by those who never lost their moral path to the top.

However, many other kinds of entrepreneurs believe that it is, indeed, a jungle out there—a tough and ruthless world. For those growing up in impoverished neighborhoods where violence is the norm, this is a logical belief that the system works that way. But others who have been nurtured in comfortable and safe environments have no such excuse. For them, seeing the world as a jungle is an artificial construct that makes their unethical behavior logical. If you live in a jungle, after all, morality has no place in your life if you wish to survive. You must fight as hard as you can, outwit and deceive your opponent at every turn, and bend or break the rules altogether. Ruthlessness becomes a necessity, even a virtue. You have to get to the top and stay there while doing it by any means necessary. Thus, the idea of a world in which success and happiness may be achieved through hard work and enlightened self-interest is an anathema to the exploiter. In such an environment, his or her behavior would have no rationale. Certainly we would have no problem understanding the Mafia operating with this kind of logic, but theirs is a criminal empire, and they make no bones about it.

Robber Barons

The robber barons of post-Civil War America represent an early type of exploiter. These wealthy industrialists rationalized their exploitation of people and resources as the inevitable effects of progress—new technology, railroads, industry, open lands, immigration, and education. Steel magnate Andrew Carnegie comes immediately to mind. Born in 1835 in Scotland, his father was a weaver who was reduced to poverty when steam-powered looms, a product of the Industrial Revolution, destroyed his livelihood.

"I began to learn what poverty meant," Carnegie would later write. "It was burnt into my heart then that my father had to beg for work." And this imbued him with the resolve that he would cure this pain when he got to be a man. Carnegie's mother, a self-sacrificing tigress, pushed the family to emigrate to America, where they settled in Pittsburgh, the iron-manufacturing hub of the young country.

Carnegie was an innovator, always open to new industrial, technological, and financial techniques that would increase profits. His relations with business associates, however, were characterized by seduction, manipulation, and betrayal. He hired subordinates who fed his insatiable narcissism, and he kept them as dependent as possible—they needed him for their livelihood. He was ungrateful to those who helped him succeed, often discarding them once he no longer needed them.

But had you asked Carnegie how he viewed himself he would probably profess that he was a good man, concerned about progress and the well-being of the workers. And of course he gave freely to charities. Carnegie wrote tracts in support of the working man's rights to organize and to negotiate contracts. But in practice he grew enormously rich by developing new technology and large-scale production methods that cut costs and by implementing new management techniques that then cut workers' wages. Carnegie cornered the steel market in post-Civil War

America but in the process crushed unions and instituted production lines that stripped workers of their dignity and allocated the work to be done by semi- and unskilled laborers.

Carnegie promoted the ideals of American democracy—these ideals had, after all, allowed him to transform himself from a worker's son to a business titan. He never acknowledged that anyone had helped him, insisting that he had worked hard for every penny he made. Later in life Carnegie gave freely as a philanthropist—there are numerous foundations and buildings named after him—but that endeavor seems to have brought him little satisfaction. Thirteen years after Carnegie's retirement, he admitted that life outside the business jungle was boring. "It is the pursuit of wealth that enlivens life," Carnegie said. "The dead game, the fish caught doesn't mean very much in an hour." There was a ruthlessness about Carnegie that pertains to many other exploiters who have little feelings toward those around them. However, Carnegie never engaged in outright criminal activity. At times his behavior may have been on the border of bending the rules but never really breaking them.

Maccoby, who studied the Mexican villages and afterward turned his attention to particular kinds of business leaders in already-industrialized countries. These business leaders were different types from his previous concepts of lions and foxes. He interviewed a number of corporate managers who saw themselves as true jungle fighters. Upon further analysis, he found that these jungle fighters worshipped power and would go to great lengths to attain it. They trusted no one except their wives, who tended to subjugate their lives to their husbands' quests for power. They to make others feel valuable as long as they were of use, only to drop them after their usefulness was at an end. These jungle fighters exhibited a tremendous sense of entitlement that allowed them to break rules, but not laws, that were surely only meant for lesser mortals. They were not that concerned with whom they might hurt in the process.

To study Marc Dreier's life is to receive an education in what constitutes the perverse pathology that typifies the jungle fighter as an exploiter. Dreier was a man who had everything going for him: superior intellect, analytic ability, and ambition. Sadly, Dreier's compulsion to engage in deceitful, manipulative conduct was also way above average. In the end the exploiter in him became so dominant that he now has twenty years of prison time to reflect on the damage he has done and the lives he attempted to destroy in the process.

Marc Stuart Dreier

Marc Stuart Dreier was born in 1950 and grew up in Lawrence, Long Island, one of the fabled, affluent "Five Towns." His father was a captain in the Polish army, who, assigned to the New York World's Fair in 1939, found himself marooned in America by the start of World War II. He stayed, married, and went on to open a string of movie theaters in Manhattan and on Long Island. The elder Dreier retired to Florida in the 1970s, but unable to adjust to retirement, he started a second string of theaters that Marc's brother, Mitchell, runs today. The family was seen as close, loving, and protective of one another.

From childhood Marc was viewed as a golden boy. He attained high grades, and teachers and other students saw him as both smart and a good talker—someone destined to succeed. He set his sights on becoming a courtroom attorney, a litigator. Those who knew him the longest thought he had a selfish streak—a need to always come out first—yet there was another side to him: charming, ambitious, and hardworking.

He got into Yale, earned a degree in 1972, and went on to Harvard Law School, where he graduated in the middle of his class in 1975. Afterward, he got a job as a litigator in the law firm Rosenman and achieved a fair amount of prominence. He was a hard worker, grinding through one hundred-hour weeks, and he was admired for both his skills and his work ethic. By 1985 his hard work paid off, and he was made a partner. And around that time he began dating an attractive Rosenman associate named Elisa Peters. They married in 1987 and had two children, a boy and a girl.

However, his firm did not prosper, and he became incensed that he was having trouble getting new clients. He found that the older lawyers jealously guarded their clients, and he grew restless. Even after he was made partner, he found that the bigger salary and responsibility didn't really change that much for him. In fact, nothing really changed that much except that he grew more irritated and annoyed with his plight. This attitude followed him throughout his life. Every shift in good fortune eventually ended up in more frustration.

Dreier felt that his anger was caused by the frustrations heaped upon him, and he was able to point to those factors that operated in reality but not to any underlying character traits. The firms he worked for went through changes, which he saw as working against him. But what really worked against him was this overly idealized version that he constructed about himself. His fantasy was to own some grand apartment with the finest paintings that would adorn his walls. He felt that he had to create an image that would impress not only potential clients but probably the rest of the world. He had such a sense of his own importance and a need to impress and project himself as an imposing figure. The trouble was that he just never made enough money to cover that lifestyle. It was so out of proportion with who he actually was.

This expansiveness, the need to enlarge his life and to impress others, led him into activities that eventually drove him to engage in deceitful pursuits. Becoming rich was a passion, a driven need, and it really didn't make any difference to him how he would attain this. As we followed his life and the many devious paths that he took, it became clear that his view of the world was a bit skewed. When he looked out, he saw the human race as one that appeared to resemble living in a jungle, albeit a hostile environment. He treated others ruthlessly, damaging careers and life savings along the way. He viewed his fellow contemporaries as possible prey for him. Like the lion, he carefully worked out methods of attack that unfortunately involved lying and various kinds of fraud, such as forging financial documents or assuming other identities to fool investors. At this point the only thing in his life that spurred him on was to make more and more money to support his bloated lifestyle. There could be no turning back and taking on a more modest role for himself; his mind had given itself over to a life of deception and scheming—an out-and-out con artist. Now he had to exploit whatever he came into contact. Nothing was sacred.

Every unfortunate experience seemed to become a metaphor for his own life. He saw the tragedy that befell the World Trade Center as a personal allegory. His marriage was coming apart; in fact, he really had little interest in his wife, and she filed for divorce in January 2002. He felt as if the forces around him coalesced against him.

Type A Personality

In a book published in the 1950s there was a personality described as the type A. It was first described as a potential risk factor for heart disease by cardiologists Meyer Friedman and Mike Jordan. Later on the theory came under criticism. These criticisms included unequal sample sizes and exclusion of the female population as a whole. However, the interest here is not to validate the theory but rather to see if in the theory there are important issues that would relate to someone like Dreier.

The type A personality has something to do with being competitive and work-obsessed. These people are seen as impatient, or workaholics, and very ambitious. There is usually a sense of time urgency; they get frustrated while waiting in line, they walk or talk at a rapid pace, and they are always painfully aware of the time and how little of it they have to spare. They are said to have a short fuse.

In the overall assessment of this personality trait, one aspect of it has been overlooked. We know how these people appear; we know about their reactions in life; we can even predict their behavior to some extent. However, we haven't paid sufficient interest to what creates these conditions for these people. What exactly are they responding to, and what causes such frustrations in them? This is the part that mostly relates to Dreier.

The type A personality views the world in a particular way. It is not a world that is inviting, nor is it a world that is wide open for them to move ahead. Rather, it resembles the law of the jungle. Without realizing it they see a world in front of them that is forbidding and hostile, if not antagonistic and competitive. The more ambitious they are, the more frustrated they become because there is always a lingering feeling that they are being held back or that their progress is impeded. The gates of life are not open, but rather they must exert much force to push open these gates. This view leads to an experience that their progress is constantly being obstructed or impeded in some way. With this in place, the type A is always on the look out for devising methods to overcome this predicament. We see them at a check-out line in a grocery store, and when the line slows down, they become furious if not frantic. Waiting is one awful experience for the type A.

Dreier recounts the following experience. He had a home in the Hamptons that he still continued to go to after his marriage breakup. One weekend day while taking a walk along the beach—his home was inland—he spotted a great house that abutted the beach. The house took on such an aura of opulence, the very thing he felt he needed to store up his fractured ego. He realized then that he must buy a house on the beach—that doing so would resurrect his life. To afford this he knew that he must expand his firm that he had started and rename it, Dreier LLP. But he needed the money to pay for this new venture. As he said, "I wanted to just, well, appease myself, if not gratify myself. I was very, very caught up in seeing the criteria of success in terms of professional and financial achievement, which I think was a big part of the problem. But I thought it would make me happy. And I wanted to be happy again."

He was such an outstandingly self-centered person. His own interests, desires, and impulses were the one and only meaningful core of his existence. Now his true nature emerged. Ideas of mutuality, of sharing, of devising strategies to surmount these failures were beyond his imagination or even temperament at this time. He knew only the "book meaning" of the words. As he saw it, he had to take off his gloves and fight as hard or as dirty as he needed. Of course, all of this was rationalized so that he felt entitled to lead the kind of life that would bring him to the riches he felt that he deserved and that, in addition, should have been coming to him. From businessman to predator, from lawyer to exploiter. Whatever wins was what he would pursue without regard to the consequences.

Now the big question reared its ugly head. How in hell was he going to pay for all of this? And thus began his journey into a life of fraud, exploitation, and an even more distorted reality. He was desperate to find a solution, and he had an irrational overconfidence in himself. He felt he could will himself to do anything that his heart desired. To do this he kind of knew that he had to cross the boundaries into illegal behavior. He said that he felt as if fraud would be a onetime event that was necessary to fuel his expansive plans. Once out of his present financial crisis, he would then go back to the other side of the boundary and once again play by the rules. However, he admits that initially he really didn't have that much of a psychological struggle crossing the line of ethical behavior.

He was consumed with the problem of his finances. We need to look a bit closer at what he was going through and how he decided to resolve this conflict over finances. His problem was not just that he could deviate from normality, playing by unethical rules. But more to the point, it was about the ruthless pursuit of achieving a goal that was outside of his range of ability or skill. So he needed to enter into a new phase of his existence. He knew he had no choice other than to deceive others, to lie to them, and to lead a life of fraud. He acknowledged reality, knowing what he was planning to do was criminal. Yet, oddly enough, at the same time he was able to deny in his mind what he was doing. Reality threatened his self-interest, which would have meant either shelving his plans for expansion or trying to raise money in a legitimate way. In essence, he destroyed the connection between truth/reality so that he was able to live a life as a con artist. Two sides actually existed within him. On the one side of his personality, he was able to see things for what they were or as others saw them, but on the other side, his personality was locked in a delusion that gave him permission to act on his wildest fantasies. He told himself in a halfhearted way that he could always work things out if he had to. In essence he said to himself, "This is who I am; this is what I deserve, and I have every right to get it."

Splitting

In psychology, we call this process one of *splitting*. Dreier's mind is split into two parts that exist independently of one another. This is a primary psychological defense that enables him to live within these two sides. The deluded denying side can always make claims upon him because he realizes that there is no realistic way that he can raise the money he needs. However, that reality is unacceptable. That reality has to be rejected. It is too threatening because it means that he must deprive himself of those wonderful homes and other expensive possessions. Driven by his own self- interest, knowledge remains the slave of desire rather than the companion of reality.

Dreier's sense of powerlessness frightened him. The fear is not simply that others might think he is weak and ineffectual but that he might actually be weak and ineffectual. His sense of powerlessness is overdetermined it can be traced back to childhood traumas where he actually believed in being powerless once, and unfortunately this fear followed him into adulthood. His decision to enter a life of exploitation represents a triumph over the barriers and boundaries that held him in a position of failure. This failure is intolerable, and so he just collapsed his hold on ethical principles. This is the solution undertaken by all kinds of con artists. Of course, we do have room for corporate cowboys who, through their creativity, bring forth fascinating ventures, but we do not have room for those who later make mistakes, especially in their risk-taking, and step over the ethical line and then attempt to cover up their mistakes. Dreier didn't merely decide to bend the rules; he knew he had to break the rules completely.

Dreier then started on a program that would enable him to amass the money he needed. He realized that once you cross a gray line it's much easier to cross a black line. His idea to commit fraud was rationalized as a one-time event that was necessary to fuel his overblown plans. He saw hedge funds as his prey together with the hedge-fund billionaire managers who were eager to throw around investment money.

Once he forged signatures on notes there was no stopping him. All boundaries could be broken. The exploiter in him was in the process of destroying the social order and constructing a new reality. Dreier's individual psychic defense of denial and his wish or assurances seemed basic to the abolition of boundaries. His perverse state of mind canceled out any sense of uncertainty because now in his mind anything was permissible—he was finally free to pursue his goals. In corruption, individual forms of morality overtake and replace culturally established forms. Corruption breeds corruption, and reality becomes distorted because parts of it are unbearable. He created an illusory reality, and a whole social context was created and took over. A key feature in this was the presence of a manufactured identity. The dynamic involves a desire to quite literally get out of a painful body or psyche. A particular set of knowledge—that which is criminal—was rejected, and now the exploiter in him must create a new, more pleasurable version of himself.

His plan was to sell an IOU, a one-year note with an interest rate of 8 or 9 percent. But it would have to come from a bogus investor. The issuer would have to be seen as an attractive, successful firm, someone who would be exciting to hedge funds. It certainly would be better, he thought, if the issuer was someone private so that the investors would not have easy access to them. The more Dreier thought about it, the more he realized that one of his richest clients, Sheldon Solow, would be the best person to issue a fake debt.

Solow was a very successful builder, well known for building 9 West Fifty-Seventh Street. He was a cantankerous eighty-one-year-old Brooklyn-born developer with a good reputation, and he was renowned with plenty of money. In fact, in 2008, *Forbes* named him the world's 605th richest man, with a net worth estimated at $2 billion. Some years before, Dreier had argued his first case for him. He was a dream client, a deep-pocketed billionaire who had an appetite for corporate combat. Whenever Solow went into battle, Dreier led the charge. Solow was always suing one person or another, and he hired Dreier to attack the other side. An attorney for the other side when asked about Dreier said that he was a combination of great intellect and complete sleaze. He was brilliant at devising alleged conspiracy theories, but his arguments absolutely made no sense.

What he did was to construct a fake Solow financial statement that he could show to other hedge funds. He looked at financial statements of similar firms and duplicated them. He knew Solow's auditor and placed the fake financial statements under the auditor's letterhead.

His first bogus transaction was for $20 million. It was a note that inferred that Solow needed the $20 million to expand, and to his surprise, a Connecticut hedge fund named Amaranth, run by a trader named Nicholas Maounis, bought it. Dreier was impressed that it came off so easily. And like that Dreier walked off with $20 million. He used it to hire more lawyers and build out more office space, and then he bought a beachfront home that he had dreamed of, a sprawling mansion in the Hamptons. Dreier felt that with this one transaction he would stop it all and that he wouldn't engage in fraud again. Oddly enough, as one could have predicted, he wanted and craved more. Now he had fifty lawyers under him who had large salaries. He was now king of the universe, and when meeting him at his office, the opulence of it impressed everyone. Who would not think that this guy was something!

After the first $20 million, Dreier quickly sold a series of additional phony notes in amounts ranging from $40 million to $60 million, eventually totaling roughly $200 million. He kept track of all the sales in a series of small black notebooks. This new reality really became ushered in with a bang. He now added a second waterfront home in the Hamptons. He drove an Aston-Martin for fun, while a chauffeur ferried him around Manhattan in a Mercedes 500 for work. He laid down $10.4 million for an apartment in New York. And then came the topping on the cake: he purchased an $18 million yacht, the *Seascape*, which he kept docked in St. Martin. It came with a crew of ten and a Jacuzzi. By the end of 2006, his law firm had doubled in size to more than one hundred lawyers. By the end of 2007, there were 175. His offices then expanded, eventually taking up eleven floors at 499 Park Avenue.

His expansiveness knew no bounds. He then went on an art-buying spree, shelling out $40 million to fill the firm's walls with Hockneys, Warhols, and Picassos. Some clients wondered how someone could spend $10 million on a piece of art and hang it in the receptionist area. Some thought that Dreier was going to outrageous attempts to glorify himself and impress everyone. It was not difficult to see that some neurotic, almost obsessed need for aggrandizement was at work. It impressed others as an obsession—he just could not stop himself. He was in overdrive and needed to take in and accumulate more and more.

Then in 2006, he decided to hire celebrity lawyers who had clients such as Jay Leno, Rob Lowe, Andy Pettitte of the New York Yankees, and singer Diana Krall. His start-up costs were enormous. Many of the lawyers had guaranteed salaries of $41 million or more. He then needed more space, and he renovated office space in the Century City skyscraper, which alone cost him an estimated $300,000 a month. Obviously, he could not stop there, and he joined country clubs, which ran him $180,000 a year to play golf. Then he opened a branch of a sushi restaurant called Tengu, and most nights he dined there surrounded by attractive young women and potential clients.

However, as one could have predicted, life took an unfortunate turn for him. He forgot that what goes up must eventually come down. The markets continued to go south, eventually leading to the collapse of Bear Stearns in March 2008. After that, almost every hedge fund refused to renew their contracts; all they wanted was their money back. Dreier realized how impossible this situation was for him; it amounted to a full-blown crisis. Almost all his outstanding notes were coming due that fall. During walks on the beach in the Hamptons, he confronted the unthinkable: $48 million of notes in September, another $15 million in November, a whopping $100 million in December, plus $60 million in January 2009. All told, he would need almost $225 million to cover these redemptions. In an old movie played by Laurel and Hardy, there is a scene where Laurel looks directly into Hardy's eyes and says to him, "What a pickle you have gotten us into." This is exactly what Dreier could have said to himself along his beach walk—what a pickle he was in.

But you can't count Dreier out; he was one resilient dude—nothing really deterred him, and he always was able to come up with new solutions. He was into this scam so way over his head that actually there wasn't much opportunity to do anything other than seek out new clients. There were clients in the Persian Gulf with enough oil money who could inject awesome sums into his firm. So after Labor Day, he began his sales push. Initially no one wanted to buy anything; they only wanted to sell. So he offered notes that were due in less than a year that would earn 12 percent that had to be repaid the following May. He did sell a small note, for $13.5 million, to a hedge fund named Veriton and then sold a note for $100 million to a fund named Elliott Associates, a $10 billion fund run by a lawyer turned money manager. All told these two sales raised half the money he needed.

Dreier's pathology includes one area in which many might envy: he is low in anxiety, especially in situations of stress or threat where most people would commonly suffer undue tension and apprehension. The rest of us may agree that worrying is wasteful and pointless, yet we find this knowledge does not spare us anxiety-stressed situations. Someone like Dreier could carry on as well as he could because he did not experience panic—certainly an advantage in such situations. But we really cannot view this as courageous but merely downright fearless—the truly brave being those who act against what they are afraid of doing.

As the markets went south, investors more and more started wanting their money back. Now Dreier's fraudulent behavior became overworked. He even resorted to impersonations. From there the dominoes kept toppling. Another client, Fortress, needed some of their money to pay creditors, and they started to think that Dreier may have stolen from them. Dreier continued to seek solutions to pay back the notes he issued, however. He was able to offer Fortress a $50 million note that was issued from the Ontario Teachers' Pension Plan, a massive $100 billion fund based in Toronto that had once been a Dreier client. The group from Fortress told Dreier that before they would sign the legal papers they demanded a face-to-face meeting with the Ontario Teachers' executive.

Dreier thought one good solution would be for him to impersonate the executive at the fund's offices in Toronto. He then telephoned Toronto and set up a meeting for the next day. However, at the last minute, the executive from Fortress canceled the meeting. But Dreier then set up a meeting with the Ontario Teachers' attorney named Michael Padfield whom he had never met. When he met Padfield, he discussed the possibility of selling him a note that had a good interest rate.They exchanged business cards. After the meeting Dreier decided to kill some time in the conference room. As he paced the floor, he saw a man emerge from an elevator. Dreier was surprised to see Howard Steinberg, the Fortress executive who had come unexpectedly to sign the note. So they had not canceled after all, but they never announced it beforehand. Steinberg was to meet with Michael Padfield, the same attorney Dreier had just seen. Dreier rushed out to meet him, as Steinberg had never met Dreier before, and then Dreier introduced himself as Padfield. He then handed him Padfield's business card and guided Steinberg into the same conference room where he had been waiting.

The talk was going quite well until Steinberg said he needed to speak to someone he knew from the Toronto Association. He asked if Dreier knew the extension of this fellow, Tom. Dreier gave him the number of the extension, and Steinberg excused himself and stepped outside to call him. Dreier realized quickly that if he got to speak to Tom he would be told that he knew nothing about the meeting or even the note. Dreier watched Steinberg dial Tom, and then he quickly called Tom himself so he could cut off Steinberg's attempt to reach Tom.

Unfortunately, Steinberg beat him to it. When he finished the call, he came back into the conference room, and Dreier noticed that he looked suspicious. Steinberg then asked him a number of questions about personnel at Ontario Teachers'. Sensing the worst, Dreier hurriedly signed the legal papers then excused himself for a moment. But instead of returning, he headed for the elevator and left the building and ran to the airplane.

Steinberg waited for a few moments and then walked out of the conference room. He turned to the receptionist and asked her if the guy who just walked out before him was Michael Padfield. She replied, "No."

What happened next was most perplexing. Once Dreier was in the airplane, a Fortress executive called him to tell him that there seemed to be some problem. The executive did not know that Dreier was in Canada, much less that he was behind the problem. Dreier told him that he had no knowledge of this. Then another call came in, and this time it was Fortress's co-chairman, Peter Briger Jr., calling to tell Dreier that they suspected some kind of impersonation was going on. Dreier told him that he would look into it immediately.

Dreier was faced with some monumental decisions. He could have just as well flown back to New York, left the scene, and then tried to work out a better solution. For example, he could have just fled the country altogether. But what he did was really odd because instead he decided to go back to the pension fund's offices. He knew he would get caught if he came back. He knew he faced defeat, but he came back anyway. Once he was back in the Ontario Teachers' offices, an attorney asked him to wait in the conference room. Within a few minutes, security guards appeared and told him to wait for the police, who appeared not long after and arrested him. Dreier offered no resistance.

The Canadian authorities held Dreier for four days and then put him back on a plane to New York where US marshals took him into custody. He didn't bother with denials. He freely admitted to everything, the whole four long years of fraud. In all, there were eighty or more bogus notes, thirteen hedge funds, and four private investors, all totaling some $380 million. His glorious new life, the firm, and the "Dreier Model" had all been built on deception, lies, and corruption. Within days, attorneys began resigning, and then the firm soon afterward declared bankruptcy.

Dreier was tossed into a dark cell on the ninth floor of the Metropolitan Correctional Center in New York, a federal holding pen. He was shocked at the conditions of the cell. He and his cellmate, the triple murderer, had no electric light, no reading materials, no heat, and a broken toilet, which left the floor covered in urine. Each night he covered himself with a thin blanket while other inmates yelled and screamed. It was as close as one could come to living in a place that resembled an insane asylum or just plain hell. His meals were shoved through a slot, and he showered twice a week in cold water.

In reconstructing his life, it was far beyond one's imagination that this could happen to a lawyer who graduated Yale College and Harvard Law School. Following his indictment a judge allowed Dreier to return to his apartment under house arrest. He realized that even if he got twenty years in prison he would come out at seventy-eight years of age. He reasoned that his father died at ninety-one so he knew he had good genes and that he would still have some years left to live after his release.

Dreier had everything going for him, and he managed not only to throw it away but to design a life that bordered on theft, lying, deception, and fraud. He was a true exploiter who deceived clients, those who worked for him and those close to him.

It is difficult to understand his decision to go back to the offices of the Ontario Associates; what are we to make of it? Most likely there is an underlying need to get caught or essentially to get punished. What characterizes Dreier so well as an exploiter is his superficial charm and good intelligence. There was an untruthfulness and insincerity, lack of remorse for shame, poor judgment, pathologic egocentricity and incapacity for love, and a specific loss of insight.

It would seem to the layman, the novelist, and other writers of fiction, as well as to professionals in psychology, that a man like Dreier would be a source of extraordinary interest. There is an aura of the sinister and the uncanny about him. How are we to explain this fascination? The interest in some people, perhaps, is mixed with fear and curiosity as in the fascination with vampires, werewolves, and Frankensteinian monsters. An individual who lacks a vital element of human normality and yet who is clearly more human than animal is deviation enough to arouse some anxiety in some people. Even if we accept that Dreier differs only in degree from the normal, it is still true that this difference is large enough and may in effect approach a difference *in kind.*

We may encounter someone like Dreier—someone notably self-centered, detached in personal relationships, conspicuously hard or cold, with perhaps a touch of the predatory manner—without knowing it. Or we might get clues that he or she is close to someone with this kind of deviant personality.

When the more threatening features of such a person are less in evidence than usual, he or she may be regarded as basically a noncon-formist to conventional standards and values, a "free spirit" who does things that others might wish to do but are withheld by fear, or thoughts of social disapproval, or "conscience." While abnormal, they are neither mentally deficient nor deranged in the usual sense. They can arouse curiosity as "the most interesting animal in the human zoo" when they exhibit exaggerations, sometimes spectacular. However, while we may disapprove or deplore the deviations, they also may be striking enough to intrigue us. A wolf is more interesting than a sheep, and certainly the deviant may have excessive color and verve. However, in the end when deviants stoop to defrauding us, they usually lose this interest and we are left hating them. Otherwise they may be one of the more interesting animals in the human zoo.

Tom Wolfe wrote a book, *The Bonfires of the Vanities,* and talked about the main character as one of the 'Masters of the Universe.' Such masters acknowledge no limits whatsoever. They have left all morality behind in pursuit of the vanities of money and status, and they believe they are entitled to everything. As in the movie *Wall Street,* the finan-ciers' only goals are money and power, with no attention to morality or care for anyone else. The characters seem shallow, with little emotional interior.

This certainly is a fair description of Dreier. He was consumed by greed for more and more, without limits. He was emptied of human emotions and treated himself and others like the commodities in which he traded. He regarded himself as more or less a well-oiled machine who had the inalienable right to achieve his God-given ends of money and power and to appear shallow and devoid of any inner psychological reality. His inner reality had been emptied out and split off, and then it totally identified with the culture of money and power.

Dreier was able to turn a blind eye to what he was doing. This behavior occurs when we seem to have access to reality but choose to ignore it because it proves convenient to do so. Steiner (1985) talks about this when he says:

At one extreme we are dealing with simple Fraud where all the facts are not only accessible but have led to a conclusion which is then knowingly evaded. More often, however, we are vaguely aware that we choose not to look at the facts without being conscious of what it is we are evading. These evasions may lead to a sense of dishonesty and to various manoeuvres which deny or conceal what has happened by creating a cover-up. (p. 161.)

What Dreier was able to do was turn a blind eye and engage in mass denial where he was able to shut out reality and wrap himself more and more into his delusion about who he needed to be. Yet, of course, this did not prevent reality from obtruding. It is interesting that he knew at some level where he was heading but would not face up to it until the end came and punched him in the face.

Chapter Three

We Are on the Frontier and We Are the Smartest Guys
Enron and the Outlaws

There once was a town in the Old West called Preyville. Over the years its population grew and prospered. Law and order was established, and a feeling of safety prevailed. This was a slow process, but the town thrived, fueled by industrious, law-abiding citizens. It was a success story that helped add to the culture of a thriving country.

One day a group of men who looked like former outlaws rode into town with their six-shooters strapped to their sides. The town elders, fearing the worst, met the newcomers and asked them what their intentions were. The men swore that they had given up their lawless behavior and that their only goal was to live in harmony with the rest of the town and hopefully participate in its economic growth. The council was impressed and actually saw something smart about them and finally welcomed them when their fears subsided.

Soon after their arrival, the former outlaws began to buy into a number of businesses and planned a real estate strategy. They bought plots of land, built homes on them, and then loaned townspeople money to purchase them. The men also bought the local bar and immediately raised prices on the whiskey. They were seen as very industrious, hardworking, and successful. While not always liked, they were respected and in some ways admired.

In the short run, the town's economy benefitted. But soon problems started to emerge. Some families who had bought the newly built homes found they could not afford to make mortgage payments and their homes went into default. Patronage at the local bar fell off because of the higher prices. In response the outlaws, who were now, in effect, running the town, found ways to disguise some of these losses in order to the keep financial picture of Preyville looking rosy. The outlaws were quick to pick up on the negative impression they were emitting and then lowered whiskey prices and eased up on the mortgage loans. The town renewed their good impression of them.

Hearing of the economic upswing in Preyville, a nearby town sent a group of elders to see the town for themselves. So they made an appointment to meet with the Preyville council. The first thing they did was look over the books. What they found was alarming: page after page of defaults on homes built by the newcomers. Even though many of the defaults were enforced, it still was frightening.

"Something's wrong here," said the leader of the delegation. "You have a lot of properties making no money. How are you able to show a profit?"

Preyville's mayor replied, "We may not be able to show profits in the present, but we hope to in the future."

"Heck," said the other man, "profits are monies collected in the present. What the future holds is anybody's guess."

"We don't see it that way," Preyville's mayor replied. "The important thing is to remain positive."

Undeterred, the man continued. "I also see that the town is buying some of these houses to make it appear as if there is high demand for these homes. This doesn't look right, and it just doesn't sit right for us. I think it's time for us to go; I don't see what we can learn here, and I wouldn't want to be in your position for no money."

After the delegation departed, the mayor of Preyville went to the town council and related the conversation he had with the mayor of the other town and the possible emergence of a critical problem they could be facing that could eventually lead to bankruptcy. After a heated discussion, the council decided to confront the men. They went over the books and the bleak financial picture that was created. The discussion turned into an argument; both sides attacked the other. The council became irate, and the mayor told the newcomers to saddle up and get the hell out of town: the council told them that the former outlaws' way of doing business was not wanted there.

The mayor told a meeting of the townspeople that he was sorry that he didn't act sooner but that he had been afraid of facing this bleak picture. Now they were forced to face it.

The outlaws then conferred among themselves and decided to pocket whatever profits they had and get out while the going was good. Taking stock after the outlaws' departure, Preyville found that their former prosperity had been severely compromised. The town was now beset with economic problems.

As one citizen muttered, "It seems as if we have to start all over again, but hopefully we can learn from this experience. No one wanted to face the problem head on, so we all deluded ourselves. That will never work; it is just like a cancer that affects everything around it."

The Frontier Mentality

It's important to remember that expansion is part of what made the United States a great power. Our country's westward movement in the nineteenth century exemplified the adventurous, can-do qualities of Americans. It provided new opportunities for the country's burgeoning population and helped define the American character. An economic revolution was in the making. The opening of the Western frontier brought with it a vitality that helped move this country to the forefront among the nations of the world.

The push west also had a profound effect on the world view of the adventurous souls who undertook such journeys. The frontier mentality emphasized self-reliance and a belief in endless possibilities for those bold enough to pursue them.

But there was a less attractive aspect to this mindset. At the beginning, frontier life was far from idyllic. An ethos of lawlessness and a contempt for order led the strong to dominate the weak, exploiting and sometimes destroying them. Mankind's worst impulses were on display. Over time towns established a system of law and order, the outlaws were subdued, religion had provided a civilizing force, and deputies and marshals were able to establish a safe and secure environment.

The frontier created a need for railroad lines, new goods, and production systems as the nation pushed toward the Pacific Ocean. Industries producing a variety of goods were established to keep the expansion moving. Trade with other countries flourished.

Today, although the physical expansion of the United States has been achieved, the frontier mentality of Americans remains. The person who stops expanding his or her existence—whether in the psychic or economic sphere—is thought to emotionally shrink. His or her life force begins to ebb. What is left is a monotonous external and internal landscape.

The development of an individual or a nation also applies to a business. The successful ones are always expanding and always looking for new ways to market their goods and new personnel to lead them in this pursuit. The person at the helm—the chief executive officer—is crucial to a firm's progress. A CEO who keeps a company's stock heading north is seen as a wizard and is lavishly compensated.

Problems occur, however, when a CEO begins to operate in a reckless and semi-criminal fashion. When CEOs disregard company guidelines and federal and state commerce laws—or turn a blind eye when their subordinates do the same—individuals at the top will make tons of money, but the company and the employees who have toiled faithfully in its service will be fatally compromised. Unfortunately, this is the story of Enron: the frontier mentality caught up with them.

The Case of Enron

Near the end of its existence, Enron resembled a lawless Western frontier town. Instead of a giant tilted "E," their logo should have been a blazing six-shooter. Filmmakers know that violence and lawlessness are what audiences—particularly male audiences—crave. Hollywood knows more about the inner nature of *Homo sapiens* than any political, philosophical, or scientific school on earth. Men take deeper delight in weapons than they do in women. And in Enron there was a metaphoric weapon that pervaded the business at hand. A certain kind of six-shooter mentality emerged, and the central players kept pumping away with their guns. At the height of its power, Enron's level of macho arrogance had grown to the point where you could almost hear the principles yelling, "Ride 'em, Cowboy!"

The progression of Enron as it grew from a small Texas utility trading natural gas to an international company "trading almost anything that could be traded" (Fusaro, C. & Miller 2002) can be read as a case of greed, corruption, deception, and subterfuge among its senior executives. They were corrupt but really didn't choose to see it that way, nor did they want to understand the implications of their actions. In particular, the practice of creating "special purpose entities" (SPEs) to finance

Enron's deals while keeping the debts they incurred off the company records was a fascinating tactic, obviously devised to give the appearance that the company was rolling in big bucks. Once the top brass found how easy it was to do this, nothing could stop Enron's share price from pole vaulting to the top. The executives gained personally through buying shares when the company was in the chips and cashing out when things started to go south. Raising the share price became the priority at the expense of actual growth. Through their expertise in utilities markets, Enron staff learned to create markets with themselves as the traders. They would buy gas and later electricity through the Internet and sell to distributors. Very simply, the further Enron moved away from their initial area of expertise, the less they understood the markets they were creating and the more they suffered real losses, which then had to be hidden. In short, they were out their league but found that they could play the game by concealing the real score—not an easy task in sports but very possible in the business world.

There was an enormous amount of activity buying and selling Enron's stock because both the buyers and most of the company itself believed in this illusion. The stock zoomed upward until the illicit practices were exposed. What followed was a steep and rapid descent into bankruptcy.

Not everyone turned a blind eye. Sherron Watkins, an executive, sent a memo to top executive Kenneth Lay warning him that the company was constructed on a house of cards and that its inevitable collapse would affect shareholders—many of them longtime company employees who had such faith in Enron that they had invested most or all of their money in Enron stock. Near the end, senior executives, including Lay and his lieutenant Jeffrey Skilling, foresaw the firm's imminent demise and started dumping millions of dollars in stock—all the while assuring their employees that the firm was in sound shape.

But in the beginning, when the company seemed like it could do no wrong, Lay affirmed that the driving force behind the success of Enron was the belief in free markets—and markets had not been so free since the years leading up to the stock market crash of '29. After that Congress passed legislation that kept corporations' more voracious appetites in check. But with Ronald Reagan's election in 1980, deregulation became the rallying cry of free-marketers. By the early 2000s, the Wild West had returned, albeit in corporate form. Cole Porter's song "Anything Goes" could have been the anthem for the age.

Lay took this ethos to new heights. In the mid-1990s, the SEC approved Enron's use of an accounting practice known as mark-to-market (Fusaro & Miller 2002). This allowed the firm to book projected profits on unrealized ventures as current assets. Additionally, loans made to Enron were booked as profits, flying in the face of every legitimate accounting practice. It didn't help matters that Arthur Andersen Corporation, a venerable and respected accounting firm, colluded with Enron to maintain the illusion that the company was thriving.

Perhaps it was the Lord's work Enron was doing as it pushed electricity deregulation through the 1990s. After all, what better sign of the Almighty's favor could there be than Lay's compensation for the Year of Our Deregulated Lord 2000: $141.6 million—a full 184 percent increase over his 1999 paycheck. Blessed indeed are the market makers!

What had changed so radically in the company was that the leaders substituted self-aggrandizement for honest dealing. At its high point, Enron was seen as stabilizing the US gas markets and expanding gas production nationwide. To their own way of thinking, Enron's leaders were not crooks but visionaries engaged in transforming American industry.

"We're on the side of angels," Skilling told *Business Week* (1998) a little while before. "In every business we've been in, we're the good guys." However, according to *Enron: The Smartest Men in the Room*, a chronicle of the rise and fall of the firm, these self-professed good guys engineered and created rolling blackouts up and down the state of California in order to artificially inflate energy prices.

This state of affairs, however, could not last forever, and in 2001 Skilling, then president of Enron, took on the CEO role following Lay's resignation after failing to show true profits on demand. Skilling himself resigned months later. In the meantime, both men had sold massive shares of stock, all the while assuring loyal employees that the company was in robust fiscal health.

The company may have promised to deliver greater "transparency" to energy markets, but upon inspection its own affairs turned out to be a tangled mess of lies, nepotism, and exaggeration that included the overstatement of profits by some $586 million—a revelation that caused panic among investors and a catastrophic collapse for the mighty energy trader.

Enron's downfall was directly related to its corporate ideology—a zealous, cult-like love of free markets. According to an article in *The Wall Street Journal*, Enron fought fiercely and paid lavishly through its lobbyists on Capitol Hill to limit or abolish federal oversight of its trading business. It's no coincidence when those who ran ads mocking government regulators and saluting themselves as free-market mavericks turn out to be engaged in literal rule breaking and regulation circumvention. But then why should anyone feign surprise? Many—including those whose job it was to oversee Enron's activities—could or should have seen it coming for some time.

Enron was the poster child for those who believed in the almost mystical power of free markets. Examining its downfall is as good a place as any to take stock of the deregulated, privatized state into which the public had been so rudely hustled over the last decade. And here is what it looked like: Top management walking off with hundreds of millions of dollars while employees lost their jobs, investors lost millions, and customers got to look forward to more rolling blackouts. Profiteering. Bought politicians. Stock market bubbles that inevitably burst. Workers thrown out on the streets. Left to its own devices, this is what the free market does.

Ultimately the most remarkable aspect of this tawdry corporate tale is the way Enron persuaded the world that its passion for free markets, particularly in the field of energy, was somehow equivalent to "revolution," to "creativity," to human freedom itself.

For management gurus, Enron was a particularly hallowed operation. Once a simple natural gas pipeline concern, Enron turned itself into an energy trader with awesome ambitions, buying and selling contracts to deliver power across the country. Who needed pipelines and power plants and other mundane physical assets in the age of the Internet? This was a new economy. In its last years, Enron branched out to become a full-blown market maker—a broker-dealer firm trading its own product. Regulation and a fixation on being a responsible corporate citizen seemed almost quaint and—*Holy shit!*—just look at those profits!

In Gary Hamel's admiring 2000 book, *Leading the Revolution*, Enron is characterized as a "revolutionary" company, the home of "radical ideas," which "come from radical people," where "new voices have the chance to get heard." Before Enron's troubles reached a crisis point, Hamel and his hero Lay were even scheduled to appear together at a high-profile November guru-fest called the "Revolutionaries' Ball." Enron's own TV commercials exhorted viewers to ask the "confrontational" question "Why?"—a query that supposedly had the power to "bring years of conventional assumptions to a jarring halt." The company even equated its quest for free markets with the doings of visionaries like Gandhi, Lincoln, and civil rights protesters. Amazingly, the company stopped just short of including Jesus in that august group.

Ken Lay, however, was not so modest. "I believe in God, and I believe in free markets," Lay told the *San Diego Union-Tribune.* "What's more," continued this titan of the energy business, "Jesus himself was something of a '90s-style libertarian: He wanted people to have the freedom to make choices."

Those who should have known better joined in the "Hallelujah" chorus. In April 2000, *Fortune* magazine likened Enron to Elvis Presley who shook up the staid 1950s with his vibrant brand of rock 'n' roll. It is hard to believe this passage appeared in a respected business publication, so I reproduce it here in full:

Imagine a country-club dinner dance, with a bunch of old fogies and their wives shuffling around halfheartedly to the not-so-stirring sounds of Guy Lombardo and his All-Tuxedo Orchestra. Suddenly young Elvis comes crashing through the skylight, complete with gold lamé suit, shiny guitar, and gyrating hips. Half the waltzers faint; most of the others get angry or pouty. And a very few decide they like what they hear, tap their feet...start grabbing new partners, and suddenly are rocking to a very different tune. In the staid world of regulated utilities and energy companies, Enron Corp. is that gate-crashing Elvis.

The adulation persisted almost up to the end. The cover of the September 2000 issue of *Business Week* sported a photo of Jeff Skilling giving the reader a big finger-over-lips "Shhhhhhh!"

The ostensible "secret" Skilling wanted to keep, according to the article, was that the "Revolution Lives." Yes, the dot-coms were going bust through a combination of hubris and magical thinking on the part of venture capitalists, but what of it? Enron's metamorphosis into a "virtually integrated company" offered "glimmers of a possible future."

What about those Smartest Guys in the Room?

It's too simple to explain the massive corruption and fraud that took place at Enron as a freak event. A more accurate assessment is called for—an explanation of how the company's perverse and illegal activities could have gone on for so long.

Certainly, Enron's standard operating procedure flew in the face of standard business practices. Greed and arrogance have always had a place in successful companies. But in this case, it was a communal sense of entitlement that resulted in the inability to distinguish between organizational and personal ends. When people use the company's plane as a vehicle for personal use, they have overstepped the boundaries of proper business practice. When such activities are sanctioned by the top guns, they become, in effect, rules—the new normal.

Enron had a powerful enabler in this process: the accounting firm of Arthur Anderson. When Anderson gave the corporation a clean bill of health, Enron was off and running. In the year 2000, Andersen had received $52 million in fees from Enron. Anderson's chief auditor, David Duncan, chose to go with the flow, rubber-stamping Enron's questionable maneuvers and basking in the glow that came from his proximity to the energy giant and its go-go executives. Although Duncan had considerable misgivings about the financial picture at Enron, he went along with it. He seemed to want to be a good guy, a team player, and of course he felt enormous gratification with the amount of monies that Enron was paying Anderson. At his trial, Duncan stated that he had destroyed Enron audit documents because of rising fears of a federal investigation. Because of David Duncan's testimony, Arthur Anderson was convicted of obstruction of justice, effectively dooming the firm, and they subsequently went out of business.

Enron put tremendous pressure on Anderson to hide millions in debt. At the trial, Duncan told of unrelenting pressure placed upon him to cook the books. "Wherever he drew the line, Enron pushed that line—he was under constant pressure from year to year to push that line," according to OMIT) Toffler (2003). Duncan's career symbolizes what went wrong with the accounting firm. Emboldened by success and amply rewarded and pushed by an ever-demanding client, it is theorized that Duncan chose to go with the flow. There was little question that he was a client pleaser. In fact, he and Enron's chief accounting officer, Richard Causey, often lunched together as well as attended the Masters golf tournament. In fact, Duncan's whole lifestyle was elevated the closer he was to Enron.

Corruption is an attack on accepted moral principles. Yet when the corruption is vast enough, it can come to be seen as a set of acceptable rules to live by. It enables the people who are conducting corrupt business practices to view their behavior as normal, even virtuous: after all, they may reason, everyone else is doing it, no one is getting into trouble, and everyone is getting rich—why should we be the only ones missing out on big paydays as well as the adulation and social status that comes with being filthy rich? Of course, when reality hit, these good guys who bankrupted the company were universally reviled and a few found new lives for themselves behind bars. But before this happened they held themselves in high regard. This certainly needs some explanation.

In 2000 the Enron Corporation declared revenues of $101 billion, making it the seventh largest corporation in the United States. Its stock had returned a 1400 percent gain for shareholders over the preceding ten years. Yet less than three years later, Enron was in bankruptcy and its chief financial officer, Andy Fastow, a chief architect of the fraud, had accepted a plea agreement that included a reduced jail sentence in return for informing on his former colleagues. He admitted to cooking Enron's books, keeping more than $45 million for himself in the process.

Six months later Kenneth Lay was charged with eleven felonies, including involvement in a conspiracy to deceive investors and employees about the company's financial condition. In 2006, never having served a day in prison, Lay died of a heart attack while vacationing in Colorado. Even though he had been found guilty, the verdict was vacated because his death prevented him from appealing it.

The Real Evil of Enron

When President George W. Bush made a public statement about the Enron disaster in 2002, he attributed the company's downfall to a "few bad apples"—as he would later refer to the perpetrators of the torture of Iraqi prisoners at Abu Ghraib. The "few bad apples" theory, however, does not explain the Enron debacle, nor does it give us any deeper insight into the psychology of the culture of corporate malfeasance that caused it.

In a comprehensive study of the evolution of Enron's corporate culture, management analysts Clinton Free and Norman Macintosh of the Queen's University School of Business in Ontario found that a significant shift occurred between the time of Richard D. Kinder's term as president from 1986 to 1996 and Jeffrey Skilling's term from 1996 to 2001.

During Kinder's tenure Enron operated with a highly effective managerial system that included transparent governance practices. Under Skilling's watch this system was vaporized. What happened?

Enron came into being in 1985 when Kenneth Lay orchestrated the merger of the Houston Gas Company with InterNorth, Inc., becoming CEO of the new energy corporation. Lay then hired Kinder to run the company for him while Lay brokered deals and curried political favor in Washington. From 1990 to 1996, Enron's earnings increased from $202 million to $584 million, and its revenue skyrocketed from $5.3 billion to $13.4 billion.

The keys to Kinder's management style were transparency, accountability, and his personal involvement at every level of the company. At regular meetings with managers and department heads, Kinder grilled them about every aspect of their jobs—and with a near photographic memory Kinder was not easily fooled. As one manager later recalled, "You could give him a budget number and explain where it came from and he'd say, 'That's not what you told me last year.' And then he'd go to his desk and retrieve the year-earlier budget and prove you wrong. It was amazing" (Fusaro & Miller 2002).

Another unit leader said that Kinder "was impossible to bullshit," and if managers "lied to him about their numbers, Rich would eat them for lunch" (Fusaro & Miller 2002).

Evil flourishes in the dark when removed from the light of social accountability, as in the deep recesses of Abu Ghraib. The first line of defense against evil, then, is transparency, open communication, and constant surveillance of every aspect of a system. Kinder—known at Enron as "Doctor Discipline"—demanded up-to-the-minute reports so he always knew who was doing what to whom and when. In turn, he had managers do the same thing with the employees under them. At every level, then, Enron was transparent and thus less susceptible to mismanagement and corruption.

In addition to running a tight ship, Kinder fostered a family-like atmosphere at Enron, displaying concern for the personal lives of his employees. He once paid travel expenses for a manager to return home for a family funeral. Practices like these tend to engender respect and loyalty.

Social Shift

But everything changed in 1997 when Skilling replaced Kinder as president. Skilling was a graduate of Harvard Business School and a fan of Richard Dawkins's influential book *The Selfish Gene* (Oxford University Press 1976). But Dawkins devotes much attention in the book to altruism. However, Skilling misread the theory to mean that evolution is driven exclusively by cutthroat competition and self-centered egotism. Enamored of the notion of "survival of the fittest," Skilling implemented a policy at Enron called the Peer Review Committee (PRC) system, known among the workforce as "Rank and Yank."

PRC was based on the presumption that people are primarily motivated by greed and fear. Skilling ranked employees on a declining scale of one to five. The formal reviews were posted on a company web page along with a photograph of the employee, increasing the potential for personal humiliation. Those who received a five in the ranking system—no matter how good their absolute performance may have been—were automatically sent to "Siberia." From that purgatory, the unfortunate fives had two weeks to find another position at Enron. If they failed, they were given the boot.

As a result of that strategy, 10 to 20 percent of Enron's employees got axed every six months, leaving those remaining in a constant state of acute anxiety. As Lay approvingly described it, "Our culture is a tough culture. It is a very aggressive culture." Charles Wickman, one of Enron's energy traders, later described the corporate ethos under Skilling this way: "If I'm on my way to the boss's office to argue about my compensation, and if I step on somebody's throat on the way and that doubles it, well I'll stomp on the guy's throat. That's how people were" (Long 2008).

Skilling's evaluation and bonus system led to a lot of frenzied behind-the-scenes wheeling and dealing between department heads and managers, who swapped review evaluation points like so many baseball cards. A manager described the PRC system as creating "an environment where employees were afraid to express their opinions or to question unethical and potentially illegal business practices."

Because the "Rank and Yank" system was both arbitrary and subjective, it was easily used by managers to reward blind loyalty and quash brewing dissent. By pitting workers against each other in this manner, PRC brought out the worst in Enron's employees: selfishness, competitiveness, and greed. Because bonuses ranged from 10 to 26 percent of an employee's take-home pay, there was considerable motivation to manipulate the ratings to boost one's rankings in the hierarchy, as well as to sabotage deals put together by other employees and departments. One executive said that the bonus system "had a hard Darwinian twist" that made "a humongous difference on Enron by instilling a competitive streak in every employee."

In one of the more egregious results of this practice, Alex Gibney, in his 2005 documentary *Enron: The Smartest Men in the Room*, played audio tapes in which Enron traders can be heard asking engineers in California power stations to knowingly shut down energy stations in order to decrease energy supplies along a particular grid, thereby boosting energy prices.

In 2000 this led to rolling blackouts in California, significant increases in energy bills, and, of course, a huge spike in Enron's stock price. When the fire season exploded in California, further disrupting the energy grid and driving prices through the ceiling, one trader could be heard on tape exclaiming, "Burn, baby, burn!"

Another by-product of the ranking system was an environment where most employees were afraid to express their opinions or to question unethical and potentially illegal business practices.

Skilling, a risk junkie in all aspects of his life, led corporate outings such as motorcycle expeditions across the ragged terrain of Baja California, reinforcing the testosterone-poisoned atmosphere of Enron's corporate environment—one that put women executives at a decided disadvantage.

What made all this possible was deregulation. It allowed traders to dispense with the need for ethics and morality and concentrate solely on maximizing profits—no matter who suffered in the process. They approached norms and rules as obstacles to be overcome by dint of cleverness and cunning.

The flouting of rules is not always a bad thing, however. Rule-breakers throughout history—the ones who challenge established wisdom—push civilization forward. But Enron's contempt for rules was different. It didn't grow out of desire to innovate, but, rather it was a desperate effort to hide unfavorable realities from Wall Street analysts whose job it was to present a realistic and reliable financial picture to investors so that they would be able to make informed decisions.

Those in leadership positions at Enron, no matter what they may have told themselves, were not out to create newer, better, and more efficient business models. Their gratification derived from success for its own sake—even when the triumphs were illusory—and from acquiring money and goods that satisfied grandiose fantasies in which such spoils placed them above the poor schmucks who stuck to a playbook.

In the major corporate scandals of the 1990s, we find that the very people who created the companies were the ones who brought them down. A failure to separate organization from one's self leads to a powerful sense of entitlement. Enron's leaders displayed a fascinating compulsion to produce the appearance of accruing untold profits even as they were bleeding money. On a conscious level they envisioned themselves as individuals of high moral standing. With this fantasy comes a feeling of being admired and loved for their abilities and successes. Such self-delusion and arrogance became the defining quality of the Enron culture. It was a mindset that ended up destroying the company's most precious resource: the creative imagination and know-how that produces actual products that improve people's lives. When a company's only goal is to create profits, its reason for existence disappears and its downfall becomes inevitable.

Ultimately the smartest guys in the room failed to distinguish reality from their subjective experience and self-aggrandizing fantasies. They used their considerable intelligence not to create a more effective environment but merely to enrich themselves. The fact that they were unable to manufacture the products they envisioned became irrelevant. Their ingenuity was put to use constructing questionable accounting practices that supported the false appearance of profitability.

The tragic figures here, however, are not the morally bankrupt six-shooters we have been discussing but the rank-and-file workers who gave their lives to Enron only to find themselves without jobs and stripped of their life savings.

That is the true legacy of the Enron exploiters.

Chapter Four

Beyond Greed
The Hunts and the Cornering of the
Silver Market

In the film *The Maltese Falcon,* a ruthless consortium of three men and a woman travel the world in search of a priceless statue: a falcon whose dull black exterior concealed priceless jewels encrusted from its head to its claws. Over the years, this falcon had passed, mostly illegally, from person to person, turning up in different parts of the world. These ruthlessly acquisitive partners deceive, betray, and ultimately kill in its quest, a celluloid testimony to naked greed.

At the end of the film, a policeman picks up the falcon—which turned out to be a replica of the real thing and therefore worthless—and says, "It's heavy. What is it?" Sam Spade, the private detective, puts his hand on the bird and replies, "The stuff that dreams are made of."

We need to look closely at any activity that is played out tenaciously with an indifference to the harm it inflicts. *Webster's New World Dictionary* defines greed as the "excessive desire for acquiring or wanting more than one needs or deserves." Greed is one of the deadly sins. It conjures up cannibalistic fantasies of taking everything in and consuming all. Greed is represented psychoanalytically by the language of orality: devouring, sucking, biting.

Some, however, see greed as a virtue as euphemized by the phrases "the profit motive" or the "entrepreneurial spirit." A case in point can be seen in the iconic movie about the 1980s, *Wall Street.* In a famous scene, Michael Douglas, portraying the corporate raider Gordon Gekko, rises at a shareholders' meeting to attack company directors for their management failures. The speech climaxes with a sermon portraying greed as a noble human emotion that benefits mankind:

The point is, ladies and gentlemen, greed is good. Greed works.

Greed is right, greed clarifies, cuts through and captures the essence of the evolutionary spirit. Greed in all its forms—greed for life, money, love, knowledge—has marked the upward surge of mankind—and greed, mark my words, will save not only Teldar Paper but that other malfunctioning corporation called the USA.

At the extreme end of the spectrum, greed is a pathology of excess that is observable in the moral life when an individual strives for too much of something for its own sake at the expense of the welfare of others. When this occurs there has been a failure in human connection. While acquisitive and aggressive behavior is instrumental in an adaptation to life, it becomes pathological when it is an end in itself. In every person that are traits that serve some social value but that become nonfunctional when they lose their social connection. Greedy people do not come to grief if their behavior remains within the confines of the social order, but when the greed becomes frantic and overworked it runs a perilous course. Then the person becomes condemned by the very behavior for which he or she was formerly applauded. Such was the fate of Bunker Hunt.

The Illustrious Hunt Brothers

In the early 1970s, Nelson Bunker and his younger brother William Herbert began accumulating large amounts of silver. By the end of 1979, the brothers earned an estimated $2 billion to $4 billion in silver speculation, with estimated silver holdings of $100 million.

Yes, the Hunts were very smart, adventurous, and exceedingly wealthy. But they should have seen a good therapist before they embarked on a quest to become the richest men in the world.

Everyone was impressed by the Hunts at the start. Their financial skills were overwhelming; their ability to size up investment strategies was impressive even if their contempt for people was without peer. They were just a bunch of great guys who would screw their neighbors without blinking an eye.

In some ways they saw themselves as the greatest gunslingers of all time. Unfortunately, if the barrel of the gun that sits in your holster reaches down to your ankle, it looks real long, but the problem arises when you are going to draw against another gunslinger. By the time you manage to get the gun out of the holster, the other guy will plug you full of bullets. In the case of the Hunts, the other guys were the regulatory agencies who were more powerful and savvy than they.

The History of Silver

In 1971 the United States completely abandoned the gold standard. The United States defaulted on its promise to foreign central banks that paper dollars could be redeemed in gold. The original default on the dollar really occurred in 1913 when the Federal Reserve was created, allowing it to print more Federal Reserve notes than physical gold was in the US Department of the Treasury. Alternatively, the default occurred in 1933 when President Roosevelt said that US citizens could no longer redeem their paper dollars for gold and that US citizens were not allowed to own gold.

Why is silver such a precious item? It certainly does not have the qualities that enticed the ancient Egyptians. In fact, they valued gold as the precious metal; however, silver is half the weight of gold and it is more practical than gold. Craftsmen have a much easier time working with silver; therefore, it is more functional and serviceable. Think of teapots, silverware, silver trays, and the term "silversmiths" all form part of the cultural heritage of a nation.

After World War II, the demand for silver rose while it was quite plentiful. Yet the price never really rose, contradicting the law of supply and demand. The reason for this was that the supply was controlled by the US government in Washington DC.

The United States Treasury bought silver wherever it was sold until the world price reached $1.29. By 1939 the Treasury was buying silver on the world market for thirty-five cents an ounce.

Around 1968 the Treasury decided against using silver in the coins it minted. It was now going to use a kind of nickel that was more practical. When the government started selling off the vast amounts of silver it had accumulated, the price still remained stable. In fact, the price remained that way for some time.

The major producers of silver are the United States, Canada, Mexico, and Peru. Silver is mined much like other minerals, but it comes from smelting it from copper, lead, and zinc. More and more silver was in high demand for industrial usage, such as for photography, engine parts, dental fillings, and other medical compounds. Yet photography consumed the greatest amount of silver.

An analyst by the name of Jerome Smith predicted that silver would continue to rise from the present price of $1.60 an ounce to $4.37 an ounce. This prediction created much interest in the silver futures market and led to a highly valued investment. Bunker Hunt became excited as he saw the possibility of making a great deal of money in buying up silver.

What caught the eye of Bunker was the thrill over speculating in silver and the play that it would provide him. The game is played according to well-defined rules. At the end of each day the trades have to be settled. For each winner there is going to be a loser. Those who own a commodity or a futures contract are called the *longs*. Those who have contracted to sell and to deliver what they actually do not possess are called the *shorts*. Now the buyers who believe the price will go up are called the *bulls*, and those who bet on the price going down are referred to as the *bears*.

The game is not expensive to get into it. A single contract represents five thousand ounces of silver. Consider that the market price stands at ten dollars an ounce, which would make the contract worth $50,000. However, delivery is not part of the game so that no one is asked to put up the entire $50,000. Instead, the investor plays on margin, so for example, if in August 1979, when the price was actually ten dollars an ounce, the margin payment would have been $2,000 per contract, which represented 4 percent of its total value. This is considerably lower than investing in stocks.

Unlike the stock exchange, commodity deals have to be settled by the end of the day so that if the price goes down, the speculator who is long will be asked for more margin. So if someone bought silver at ten dollars and it fell to nine dollars, the contract would decline from $50,000 to $45,000 and then the dealer would ask the speculator to cover the whole of the loss. Speculators can lose their entire investment in a single day. But speculators do not just buy one contract. So if a player has three hundred contracts and his additional margin on the day the price fell by one dollar an ounce, he could lose $1.5 million. Similarly, the investor who is short would pay similar sums if the price rose by one dollar, from ten dollars to eleven dollars, instead of falling the price.

Over time the markets eventually became more sophisticated and instead of buying short or long, investors bought and sold contracts in transactions known as straddles. Straddles occur when investors hedge their bets; if most of the investor's contracts show a loss in the first of the straddle, there could be a balance by a profit on a later one. Another approach—one that is filled with risk but that has an all-powerful emotional sensation—is to attempt to corner the market so that by controlling huge amounts of silver the investor is in a better position to be in command of the price. This is a very risky strategy and is bound to fail, as it had previously when investors tried to corner the gold or soybean markets and failed.

This begins the story of Nelson Bunker Hunt and his attempt to become the most powerful player in the silver market. On some level Hunt must have known that he was bound to fail—that his attempt was apt to draw in too many players who would oppose him and not permit such conditions in market volatility to take place. He ignored these signs.

When silver really caught the eye of the Hunts, they began to accumulate large amounts of it, and by 1979 they controlled such huge accounts in silver that they were heading in the direction of cornering the global market. Their earnings skyrocketed, and they potentially were able to pocket an estimated $2 billion to $4 billion in silver speculation. The powers to be could not sit back and watch this happen. The Hunts were brought up on charges by the US Futures Trading Commission. They were accused of engaging in unlawful activities and were fined US $10 million and then banned from trading in the commodity markets as a result of conspiring to manipulate the silver market. To add to this insult, the fine was in addition to a multimillion-dollar settlement to pay back taxes and interest to the Internal Revenue Service for the same period.

The Road to Cornering the Market

During the 1970s huge profits in oil allowed a few men in the Middle East and in the United States to amass more money than even King Midas ever dreamed. Financial powers began to worry about the accumulated reserves of the Arabs as it related to the commodity markets. Who would have thought that the commodity futures would serve as a vehicle for large wealth? Such a gamble on this kind of scale for such high stakes was not what the commodity markets were all about.

Milton Friedman, the eminent economist, made a statement that whatever goes wrong with the markets can be blamed on government interference. But the Hunts showed him how wrong he was. Speculators like the Hunts, together with Arab monies, created conditions that almost destroyed the markets. In the commodities futures markets, greed operates quite well.

Yes, greed and the prospect of being the richest men in the world drove the Hunts into a wild gamble. Unfortunately for the Hunts, their unwavering optimism in rising silver prices got the best of them. It seems rather obvious that markets that go up will eventually have to come down, a very basic law indeed.

Market manipulation is a way of creating an artificial price by planned action whether it be by one man or a group of men. For that reason "cornering the market" in a commodity is considered both illegal and immoral. At one point the Hunts had 77 percent of the world's silver supply, either physically held or in the form of futures contracts, and because of this they had the power to substantially drive up the silver price. While they were betting that the silver price would rise, the insiders in the financial industry started making huge bets that the price of silver would crash. This began the conflict between the Hunts and the financial insiders. This was not a fair match because no group of people could reasonably win against these insiders.

So while the Hunts started buying all the silver contracts that they could gobble up, financial industry insiders started betting against them by shorting their contracts (betting to have silver fall in price). A very frightening scenario emerged: the Hunts had bought more silver than actually existed. If the contracts were called in, then the futures exchange would be forced to default on its promise to deliver silver. It had no way to cover these contracts, and if the Hunts were successful, then the commodity exchange would collapse in default or bankruptcy. A very serious situation hung in the balance.

By January 1980 the price of silver hit a record high of fifty dollars an ounce, and at that time the Hunt brothers held nearly $4.5 billion in silver, much of it in Swiss bank vaults. Hunt defended his position: he said that they should not be blamed for this predicament because "There was probably a couple hundred thousand people that were buying silver."

When the federal commodities regulators set trading limits, the prices began to drop and the Hunts could not meet the margin calls on their futures contracts. A sell-off followed, and on Thursday, March 27, 1980, silver plummeted to less than eleven dollars an ounce.

"We were forced to sell and we did," the Hunts said. Their losses exceeded $2 billion. In one assessment, Bunker Hunt believed that apocalyptic days were approaching that would render paper money worthless. Hunt may have been a fanatic who believed in this kind of thinking.

The brothers were charged with using fraud and conspiracy to monopolize the world silver market. Hunt filed for bankruptcy and was forever banned from American commodity trading. Even at his wealthiest, he was known to wear cheap suits, drive around in aging Cadillacs, and fly coach.

"We didn't have to give up any yachts, because we didn't have any, and we didn't have to give up a butler because we didn't have one," he said.

The large banks that bet against the Hunts knew they had the advantage in this conflict; they knew that the Federal Reserve would be forced to bail them out; otherwise, the financial system could have collapsed. In short, there was no way that much silver could have been physically delivered. So the Federal Reserve saved the day. The people who sat on the boards of the regulatory body are all made up of financial industry insiders, each of whom had a huge short position in silver. So they were in a position to establish rules that could hurt the Hunts.

They restricted the number of silver contracts each person could own, and then they raised the margin requirements for long speculators but not short speculators. So then the Hunts were forced into margin calls, and the short speculators could sit back and wait to buy and cover the contracts. To add to this, the Federal Reserve jacked up interest rates so that the Hunt brothers had to meet the interest payments on their margin debt. Borrowing at 5 percent to buy silver is a bargain when inflation is 15 percent. It doesn't work so well, however, when someone is borrowing at 20 percent to buy silver when inflation is 15 percent.

In addition, the Federal Reserve told the banks to stop lending any more money to the Hunts. The Hunts needed more money because with high interest rates they were unable to make their interest payments. Following this the Hunts were hit with margin calls, and so they were forced to sell their long positions. The insiders had taken a short position so that they accrued large profits. The Hunts were left with huge positions that they had to sell off, and the only buyers were the insiders who had invested in short positions.

The Hunts were then brought up on charges of trying to corner the market in silver. By this time they had lost enormous amounts of money. They could not realistically go up against the financial industry insiders who changed the rules of the game to bankrupt them.

Obviously, it was important to bankrupt the Hunt brothers. The financial industry insiders will always be bailed out by regulatory changes or by the Federal Reserve. In this case the financial industry insiders had huge short positions. The insiders were bailed out by the regulatory changes and by the Federal Reserve jacking up interest rates, causing a temporary money supply crash.

What the Hunts had tried to do was not unique. A hundred years earlier there was a group of bankers who formed a ring with some industrialists. They planned to establish a cartel to control the copper price. By 1890 they held 160,000 tons of high-priced copper. In addition they had contracts to buy more. However, the scheme did not work; they ran into trouble that they never predicted and the price plummeted by 50 percent. The banks had to advance 140 million francs to keep the situation solvent. One of the principal organizers committed suicide.

If Bunker Hunt had one regret it was possibly that he had not succeeded in becoming the richest man in the world. He had been in 1967. And we might ask why that was so important for him.

Doug J. Swanson of the *Dallas Morning News* in March 22, 2009, interviewed Bunker Hunt, over thirty years later. He talked to Hunt about how his scheme collapsed, which resulted in a tangle of lawsuits, bankruptcy, and tax problems.

Hunt thought awhile and then said, "It was unfortunate, let's put it this way. They were gunning for us pretty hard."

At eighty-three, with the legal lawsuits behind him and the taxes paid, Hunt lives in relative modesty in a North Dallas house with his wife of fifty-seven years. During the interview he hobbled across his living room on shiny running shoes and a cane before settling down in a wing chair. He talked amiably but haltingly and complained that his memory is poor.

"No regrets," he said in response to a question. "I guess if I thought about it hard enough, I'd probably come up with some."

As for his role in the silver collapse—smallish fare by current Wall Street standards but probably the biggest financial scandal of his era—Hunt maintains that he did nothing wrong.

"I don't think anybody can corner the market," he said. "But I guess if you buy up a lot of items...the price can go up."

Such self-evident declarations are a staple of someone who once said that if a man can tell you how much money he has, then he doesn't have much money.

At that time he did have a worldwide empire that included Yemeni oilfields, Australian cattle ranches, horse farms, antiquities collections, pizza parlors, and at least one bowling alley. Though he lost his position on the list of the world's richest people, he never descended to pauperdom. The bankruptcy did not touch the trust left to him by his father. Its value has been estimated at $200 million.

These days Hunt goes regularly to his office at Thanksgiving Tower in downtown Dallas. "I'm working on some overseas oil exploration in Africa and the Middle East."

He started buying racehorses again and has won the Eclipse Award for Outstanding Breeder three times. "I've still got a few horses, yeah," he said, referring to his one hundred or so thoroughbreds. Hunt didn't have much to say about the current economic situation except that he owns a few stocks. However, one recent item in the financial pages caught his attention: the price of silver.

"It was close to thirteen bucks an ounce," he said. "That was considered a pretty good price fifteen or twenty years ago, and it's still a pretty good price."

What Drove the Hunts?

Those who are very ambitious and strive to achieve much in life often feel that they are special. The privileges they allow for themselves and their expectations relate to this idea of their "entitlement" in life. Those who inherently feel as if they are entitled to a great deal are in a better position to take from life. In this analysis there is a normal sense of entitlement and a negative sense of entitlement at the opposite end of the spectrum.

Those who have a normal sense of entitlement usually find a path that enables them to fulfill a life within reasonable limits determined by their skills and talents. Those with negative expectations usually deprive themselves throughout their lives; they set moderate limits for what they can acquire. The normals form a reasonable expectation picture of where they are going while the negatives construct a picture of unworthiness and take very little for themselves. Sometimes we look at someone, size up his or her life, and intuitively know how much that person takes for himself or herself. Those with small levels of entitlement constrict their lives, don't accumulate that much, and have narrow expectations of what they feel is coming to them. This is the lowest spectrum of entitlement. The Hunts represent the highest spectrum of this continuum.

The Hunt brothers were born into riches and from an early age were very well off. However, there are many people born this way who go on to achieve a great deal for themselves while their expectations stay within reasonable parameters of reality. Their success rests on a realistic understanding of what is attainable. Throughout history there have been many very affluent families, the Rockefellers, the Gettys, the Fords, or the Buffets and the Gates. All were amazing successes, but in looking into their lives they never exceeded what constitutes a reasonable boundary of success. They were adventurous, risk-takers, brilliant, and of course extremely ambitious. We could say that they had a high feeling of entitlement, maybe even excessive but never distorted.

The Hunts possessed a grandiose vision of their place in the world. Their underlying feeling of entitlement was fueled by an overly idealized vision of their place in the world. Grandiosity is a stage that all children go through. At an earlier time, they feel as if they are the center of the universe. That is until they realize that they need their parents for survival and then their grandiosity becomes tempered, and in this process they adapt a more realistic vision of their place in the world. However, let's imagine a case scenario where the child never gives up this grandiose vision he has of himself and he carries it forth into adulthood. This adult may begin to find himself in trouble in his relationship both to his world and to the people surrounding him.

Grandiosity has to do with a sense of inflated worth where a person labors under its yoke and will overestimate his or her own importance. Grandiose people tend to be contemptuous of others and harbor hostile feelings toward them. For example, Bunker felt contempt for those who he felt were small players in the market. He may have had a need to feel stronger or more dangerous to others. "I can be the richest or the most powerful person in the world." This may have been his mantra.

Another problem with grandiosity is that it produces a failure in empathy. The Hunts attempt to corner the silver market would have caused undue hardship to others, resulting in bankruptcy to investors. But this seemed only a minor concern to them.

Fay (*Beyond Greed*, 1982) mentions a conversation he had with a colleague who was also an expert in grain trading. The colleague remembered the Hunts' foray into the soybean market. In Chicago in 1977, Bunker and Herbert had purchased more than one-third of the soybean contracts in the market. The largest short seller was a grain trader named Cook Industries. The size of that short position bankrupted the company, and on June 1, 1977, its chairman, Ned Cook, asked that trading in the company's shares be suspended while he organized an orderly repayment of its debts.

A reporter telephoned Bunker in Dallas to ask what he thought of Ned Cook's plight.

"Is this on or off the record?" Bunker inquired.

"On the record, please, Mr. Hunt," said the reporter.

"Well," replied Bunker, "I think Ned Cook's a fine gentleman, and I'm real sorry this has happened to him."

"Off the record, Mr. Hunt, how do you feel about Ned Cook?"

"Tough shit," said Bunker.

An excessive sense of entitlement leads to other problematic issues. It can function as a defense against uncomfortable feelings, among which are envy, guilt, shame, and depression. This bloated sense of entitlement helps to overcome irrational reactions; however, once it becomes detached from early childhood emotions, it can act to distort one's place in the world. The person then feels as if he or she has everything coming to him or her. Such a great sense of entitlement creates an unrealistic picture of what is reasonably attainable. Certainly trading in the financial world where there are hopes of making excessive amounts of money is a perfect staging area for a person with a grandiose sense of entitlement. "Why not take it all?" For Dreier it would be "Why not take it all in any way possible."

There are two mental states that complement an extreme sense of entitlement. One is a sense of omnipotence, and when grandiosity gets into the mix it can cause real trouble. Omnipotence creates conditions of having unlimited power, authority, or force and will cause a person to overestimate his or her abilities. The omnipotent person starts to undertake actions that exceed his or her capabilities. Grandiosity has to do with an inflated self-worth that leads to unrealistic expectations, and a person laboring under its yoke will overestimate his or her own importance. His or her inner dialogue may go something like this: "I am dangerous to you. I am stronger than you. I am able to take more risks than anyone else" or "I can be the richest or the most powerful person in the world."

The grandiose person's pathology is illustrated in Henrik Ibsen's play *John Gabriel Borkman*. In the play we observe the title character's exquisite sensitivity to criticism, his paranoid alertness to skepticism about his extravagant claims, and his terror to being unmasked.

Borkman is an aging former bank director who has spent several years in prison for embezzling his clients' funds and ruining them in the process. According to him, he had been on the verge of a great coup with which he would have refunded the money. Once admired, he is now shunned by almost everyone except for Foldal, his former clerk. Ruined like the rest, Foldal nevertheless maintains contact with Borkman and supports his ex-boss's illusions that one day everybody will realize that they cannot do without him, that he will be vindicated, and that his former status will magically be restored. Foldal does so in exchange for Borkman's support of Foldal's illusion—that a book he has written will one day be published and he will be recognized as a man of letters.

Borkman's fragile ego is in need of constant bolstering. He is always poised to attack Foldal if he senses any doubt on Foldal's part that Borkman will indeed be vindicated or blamed for what happened. One senses in Borkman's hypersensitivity the kind of suspicious vigilance that a grandiose person may display when his feelings of entitlement are jeopardized in the relationship. We also see the danger of a kind of collusion that sometimes occurs when one deluded party wittingly or unwittingly supports the other's illusions.

While growing up we need a warm and caring environment to foster feelings of security as well as healthy stimulation in order to develop our potentialities. When these requisites are not met, a child develops an illusory and exaggerated sense of who, ideally, he or she should be and how other people should relate to him or her in order to confirm and substantiate the illusion. The more precarious these illusions are, the more they require an external confirmation of their own importance.

Their self-esteem depends on this confirmation from others so that their illusions about themselves are bolstered. Often those who have excessive feelings of entitlement feel undernourished, and they make up for this by striving to attain grand notions of what they can get or take from society. We all crave to attain a positive sense of self-esteem. In growing up we must learn to evaluate our potentialities and accept our limitations. But grandiose schemes in life represent an infantile wish to be all powerful. Having an exaggerated, unrealistic picture of who we really are often runs us into trouble along the way. We all place great importance on money, and those who have the most money see themselves in a cherished position. They really have attained the stuff that dreams are made of.

Let's take a closer look at Bunker Hunt. He was a successful investor, wealthy beyond all means, but he did not feel it was enough to satisfy these grand notions of himself. He didn't just want to be a successful investor; he wanted to attain the status of the biggest and most significant investor of all time. He was active in organizations and was quite prominent in his community. He was well respected and greatly admired for his wealth, yet all of these accolades could never be enough to satisfy his craving. He was reaching for the moon—it never was enough.

Maybe the need to boost his self-esteem overrode an underlying danger of passivity, and his exaggerated ambition was used to involve him in incessant masculine activity. No success in reality could measure up to such limitless inner demands, and so he reached out for illusory goals. This bottomless need for grandiosity is clearly something of a compensatory striving. One thinks that underneath it all, he or she needs to feel as if he or she would be the wealthiest person in the world, or at least in the United States. Compensatory narcissistic self-inflation is among the most conspicuous form of pathologic self-esteem regulation. However, attempts at this kind of compensation prove unsuccessful because they result in risky and over inflated business decisions that often result in massive monetary losses even verging on bankruptcy.

The pathology in Hunt's case rested predominantly on the grandiose content of the ideals he had set up for himself. He tried to satisfy his goal of self-aggrandizement through enormous investments where the fantasy of riches certainly outweighed the reality of being able to actually attain them. To speak of a compensatory strategy is to wonder what Hunt was trying to make up for. Why did he need to position himself as larger than life, a figure to be reckoned with, someone more than just important in the world, but someone who was *the* most important figure in life or maybe someone to be feared. He was in the position to have cornered the silver market and therefore controlled massive kinds of investment and market activity. The problem is that compensatory narcissistic fantasies often are poorly integrated into realistic adult thinking and strategies. Therefore, it was inevitable that Hunt would run into trouble along the way as he did throughout his life.

When the illusion of wealth becomes such an overriding need, the distinction between reality and imagination becomes blurred. Hunt's abandonment of reality was not the total picture of who he was, but it operated in restricted areas, especially those in high finance. Did he have to outdo his father, who was an oil tycoon? It is difficult to know what motivated him to strive for such power.

His manic self-inflated orientation had to shift when he failed to achieve his goals. His infantile value system knew only absolute power—the attainment of riches beyond anyone's imagination. It belonged to the early time in his life when he was an infant and when only black and white existed, good and bad, pleasure and pain, but nothing much in between. There are no shadings, no degrees; there are only extremes. The state of self-inflation is intensely competitive; he needed to outdo others, to gain advantages over them, to make more money and have more power to control the business of silver so that he could say to himself, "I am bigger than you—I am better—I am the best." This primitive correlation of value to size is, of course, a rather common phenomenon; this type of comparison fuels a sense of aggressive competition. He was driven to blind others with his magnificence; he rubbed in his successes. Unfortunately, his drive to amass wealth and power was so out of touch with reality that he was doomed to fail in the end. In the process to accumulate this much wealth, he made one mistake after another. The one big mistake was not to understand sufficiently the steps that his opponents could take to counter his drive. What started off as a semi-brilliant assault on market dynamics was doomed to fail because the other side held the trump cards.

Remember, he was unsuccessful when he tried to corner the soybean markets. There is no point in having small, mediocre failures. If you are going to lose, then lose big, and that's what he did.

Chapter Five

The Imposter: Fabricated Lives and Falsified Identifies
Clifford Irving and Elmyr de Hory

The imposter is a type of exploiter who assumes a false identity or identities, obviously with the aim of deceiving others. There are many forms and varying degrees of such behavior. For some it may consist of relatively minor actions, such as falsifying achievements or name-dropping. In its more extreme incarnations, it can result in jail time for breaking the law.

The imposter is driven by a host of factors. Imposters are aware that they are not the people they pretend to be but feel compelled to hide their perceived inadequacies by creating a new and improved version of themselves in order to feel superior to the mere mortals they set out to deceive. Imposters manipulate those with whom they interact and in doing so receive gratification that enhances their feelings of superiority.

Clifford Irving and Elmyr de Hory are two of the twentieth century's more notorious and colorful examples of this type. The irony in both of their cases is that, with benefit of hard work and persistence, both men might well have made names for themselves on their own merits. Instead, they chose to channel the better parts of their creativity into making names for themselves by use of elaborate ruses. The two actually crossed paths in 1962 on the Spanish island of Ibiza. Recognizing each other as kindred spirits, they became fast friends, with one eventually writing a book about the other's exploits before perpetrating a brazen scam of his own.

The two men's impostures varied significantly: Irving convinced a prestigious publishing company that he had gained access to the most famous recluse of his day. De Hory was a talented artist in his own right, but his real skill lay in creating eerily convincing works in the style of world-famous painters and tricking the art world and the public into believing they were the real thing.

There are other differences. De Hory, through his counterfeit paintings, impersonated a host of great artists. Irving presented himself under his own name but convinced some of the savviest people in the publishing world that he had skills and connections that were in fact far beyond his grasp. They were both found out in the end, but de Hory paid a heavier emotional price.

Clifford Irving

Clifford Irving was born in 1930 and grew up in New York City. After graduating from Cornell University, he married and began writing. In 1956 his first novel, *On a Darkling Plain*, was published to critical acclaim but public indifference. His first marriage lasted two years. He met his second wife, Claire Lydon, in Ibiza, and they married in 1958. Together they moved to California where Lydon was killed in an automobile accident. Irving's second novel, *The Losers,* also received excellent reviews but didn't make much money. Undaunted, Irving turned out a third novel, *The Valley.* In 1962 he moved back to Ibiza with his third wife, the English model Fay Brooke, and their sons, Nedsky and Barnaby.

Irving's fame is inextricably bound up with Howard Hughes. Born in the early 1900s into a wealthy family, Hughes was one of the most prominent figures of the twentieth century. A brilliant and eccentric man, Hughes was an enormously successful industrialist who dabbled in engineering, aviation, medical research, and filmmaking. In his younger days, he was a notorious playboy, and the national media breathlessly covered Hughes's myriad romances with Hollywood starlets.

But by the late 1950s, Hughes's eccentricities had started to bloom into a full-blown mental illness as he developed a variety of phobias that led him to become a recluse. He moved from penthouse to penthouse in the Las Vegas hotels he owned and refused all interview requests.

Irving's life intersected with that of Hughes's in a very odd way. In 1970, while in Spain, Irving reconnected with an author and old friend, Richard Suskind, who had been thinking of writing a biography of Hughes even though by this time the billionaire, whose morbid fear of germs had given rise to increasingly bizarre behavior—it was reported that he wore Kleenex boxes instead of shoes and grew out his fingernails and toenails to grotesque lengths—had not spoken to the media in years.

Together, Irving and Suskind hatched a scheme to write Hughes's "autobiography." In doing so the two banked on the fact that, having completely withdrawn from public life, Hughes would not draw attention to himself by denouncing the book as a fraud. Suskind did the research, and Irving the writing.

Irving started forging letters in Hughes's own hand, imitating authentic letters he had seen in *Newsweek* magazine. Once Irving made some headway in developing the biography, he contacted a major American publishing house, McGraw-Hill, tantalizing its publishers by saying that the eccentric billionaire had showed an interest in having Irving co-write his autobiography. Irving produced a letter, supposedly written by Hughes, to back up his claim. The book would be based on the interviews that Irving would conduct with Hughes.

Excited by the prospect of scoring a publishing coup, McGraw-Hill drafted contracts to be signed by Irving and Hughes. Of course, Irving forged Hughes's signature, and he walked out of that meeting with an advance of $500,000—$400,000 of which was supposed to go to Hughes. Irving, feeling empowered by this meeting, bargained the sum up to $765,000 with $100,000 going to Irving and the rest going to Hughes. This was the first contract that was signed.

The rest of the story is straight out of a Hollywood drama. Together, Irving and Suskind researched Hughes's life. Irving created fake interviews with Hughes that he claimed were conducted in remote locations all over the world—including one on a Mexican pyramid! The fraudsters were able to gain access to a manuscript by James Phelan, who was ghostwriting memoirs of Noah Dietrich, former business manager to Hughes. Irving was shown a copy of the manuscript in the hope that he would be willing to rewrite it in a more publishable format.

Irving did his work well: he forged Hughes's handwriting so effectively that experts declared the documents to be genuine. McGraw-Hill green-lit the project for publication in March 1972.

When word got out about the autobiography, however, many people who knew Hughes expressed doubts about the forthcoming work's authenticity. Irving bluffed that he was obliged to keep silent about the project at Hughes's express request. In the buildup to the publication of the faux-autobiography, journalist Mike Wallace interviewed Irving for the CBS news magazine *60 Minutes* and later said that neither he nor his producers had any inkling that Irving was deceiving them.

There was an enormous amount of publicity due to the fact that Hughes was such a celebrity figure and an icon of success. There had always been a world of hype around him. And now the rumors abounded about what this biography would reveal—that he bribed presidents, his different friendships with people such as Cary Grant or Ernest Hemingway, or the vivid details of affairs with movie stars such as Katharine Hepburn and Ava Gardner. The buzz about his life couldn't have been greater, and with it came the money that McGraw-Hill was willing to dole out to Irving.

There were executives at Hughes's corporation who doubted the veracity of the book. They couldn't believe that their boss would have given his OK for such a revealing account of his life. Irving must have banked on the premise that Hughes would not acknowledge whether the book was the real thing. He had been in seclusion for so long that it may have been reasonable to think Hughes would not make any comments one way or the other.

However, this would not be the case. Hughes decided to go on national radio and make an announcement. "This must go down in history," he said. "I only wish I were still in the movie business because I don't remember any script as wild or as stretching the imagination as this yarn has turned out to be. I don't know Irving."

This of course raised the specter of a wild debate. There were those, e.g., McGraw-Hill, who doubted what Hughes had to say. They had hundreds of Hughes's alleged handwritten comments, and Irving was very convincing and made a strong case that he knew Hughes so well so that whatever he had written was certainly genuine.

A number of well-known reporters swore that what they saw written had to be the real stuff, and the fact that Howard Hughes denied the whole thing only meant that his lawyers advised him to because of the large amount of money that he had given to Nixon. This certainly made sense, and it was reasonable to believe that Hughes had just gone too far in his revelations and now realized he must pull back and deny the whole project.

What made the matter even more perplexing was that handwriting experts swore that the large samples matched Hughes's handwriting. One even affirmed that it would have been beyond human capability to forge such a significant amount of material. This seemed to stick out as a real oddity because Irving was no specialist in handwriting forgery, and yet he must have had some gift in replicating Hughes's handwriting.

McGraw-Hill went forward with their plans in spite of the doubts that were raised, and they planned a first printing of four hundred thousand copies. In addition, Book-of-the-Month Club was willing to pay their highest price in history for the publishing rights.

Then the White House began to worry over what was being exposed about the monies that Hughes had given Nixon. In fact, Nixon managed to get a copy of the unpublished manuscript from McGraw-Hill and was shocked to read that Hughes had given him $400,000. How could Irving have gained any information about this sum of money? Maybe he really only guessed at it, and odd as it may have seemed, the figure was not far off the mark. The more the story proceeds the more incredible it is that Irving had such an intuition about things. In fact, his intuition had brought him to his position in life.

The advisors that counseled Hughes must have told him that this was getting out of hand and that he must do something quickly and strongly. That is when he arranged to have a telephone conference with seven journalists and then decided to televise it. It was in this conference that he denounced Irving and affirmed further that he had never met the guy. When Irving was confronted, he boldly said that the voice was a fake. At this point it almost seemed possible that Irving actually got himself to believe in the whole plot and reasoned to himself that it was the real thing. Yet at the same time he knew that he was lying and deceiving both the publishers and the public. Children are known to be able to do this sort of thing, but it is rare for adults to pull off such a distortion.

Hughes's lawyers filed suit against both McGraw-Hill as well as Irving. Irving didn't miss a trick in this whole fiasco. His wife, using the name Helga R. Hughes, deposited a sum of $750,000 in a Swiss bank. This was the sum that Irving told McGraw-Hill that he was giving to Hughes for the book. So it all seemed so well planned, but the Swiss authorities investigated the deposit and found that the person who opened the account was none other than Edith Irving. The police then went to the island of Ibiza where Irving was living. They confronted him about this, but he turned and denied the whole thing. In fact, he told the Swiss bank that they may have been dealing with an imposter.

But the Swiss bank identified Edith Irving as the person who made the deposit. At about the same time, when a certain James Phelan read some excerpts from the book, he couldn't help noticing that Irving had lifted some of the facts from a manuscript that Phelan had written earlier about the same subject. This was the end of the line for Irving; the whole ruse was exposed and his brilliant attempt to make the world believe that he was going to get at the real stuff about Hughes all went up in smoke.

By the end of January 1972, Irving realized that the con game was over. He admitted that the autobiography was a hoax. Further, he confessed that he never did meet Howard Hughes—that it all was a caper. When asked about why he did it, he asserted that he knew he could engage in careful research and together with his daring imagination felt he could pull off this exciting fantasy.

Later Hughes died while aboard a private jet flying from Acapulco to Houston in 1976. At that time he weighed only ninety pounds and was said to have become an addict of codeine and tranquillizers. In retrospect, if he would have died earlier, the whole scheme may have worked out—there would have been no Hughes to deny the story. Irving then would have been in the position to have sworn that the whole project was real, reliable, and trustworthy.

However, overwhelmed by the evidence, the Irvings and Suskind confessed their scheme, and on January 28, 1972, Irving and Suskind were indicted for fraud and were found guilty on June 16. Irving spent seventeen months in prison at the federal correctional facility in Danbury, Connecticut, and at the Allenwood Prison in Pennsylvania, where he said that the incarceration was a bonus. He stopped smoking and took up weight lifting. He returned the $765,000 advance to his publishers. His cohort Suskind was sentenced to six months and served five.

In an interview (Don Swaim, 1984), Irving said:

I had access to the secret files of *Time* magazine and *The Los Angeles Times*. I dug up unpublished memoirs and private tape recordings of conversations with Hughes. I interviewed men and women who knew Hughes intimately and had never been willing to speak to anyone about him. I grew to understand the man. The truth of a person's life is elusive and always subjective. The novelist is a kind of channeler—he can often get deeper into the subject than the historian, especially when the subject is a reclusive phantom like Howard Hughes. He was a tremendous force in 20th-century American technology and finance. His views are raw, powerful. His revelations are stunning. His life was a modern myth.

Ironically, when Irving was released from prison, he continued to write books, several of which did quite well, leaving us to wonder why Irving chose to take the path of the impostor when his legitimate work could have brought him success.

Elmyr de Hory

It is both strange and a bit extraordinary that Irving and de Hory met while living on the island of Ibiza. Compared to the scam perpetuated by de Hory, Irving appeared to be a small-timer. While Irving attempted one massive fraud, de Hory spent decades selling hundreds of paintings and passing them off as the works of world-famous artists.

A talented painter who had studied at prestigious art schools in Munich and Paris, de Hory initially found little demand for his work. In order to maintain a lavish lifestyle, de Hory decided to capitalize on his uncanny knack for emulating the style of famous artists. In 1946, according to *Wikipedia*, de Hory sold his first forgery in the style of Pablo Picasso to a British friend. Emboldened by his success, he went from gallery to gallery selling other works he claimed were by Picasso. For each painting or drawing, some of which took no more an hour to produce, de Hory could fetch between one hundred dollars and $400. None of the gallery owners questioned him—they were pleased to have the opportunity to buy such rare merchandise.

Growing more ambitious, de Hory traveled throughout Europe and South America selling his works to other unsuspecting galleries. He also mingled with the rich and famous, some of whom bought his work for their private collections.

At intervals de Hory would stop producing forgeries and instead create his own works. The forgery business had provided him with sufficient funds, and he wanted to prove that he could succeed on his own. But to his dismay, de Hory had difficulty selling his own creations, and his money rapidly dwindled. Why, de Hory thought bitterly, should he expend so much energy on his own work that just wouldn't sell when he could make hundreds of thousands of dollars selling forgeries?

In the meantime, gallery owners had begun to ask him if he had other paintings besides Picassos to sell. With that impetus, de Hory started to imitate different painters, such as Matisse, Modigliani, and Renoir, thereby expanding his repertoire. He began to charge more for his fakes. Realizing that it would be prudent to keep a low profile, de Hory began selling his paintings by mail. Now he was making a name for himself as an art dealer, and he sent letters to galleries and museums explaining that he had particular artworks that he wished to sell and including photographs of the paintings.

By then he was able to spend more of his time researching other painters, which enabled him to create works in the style of Degas, Braque, Bonnard, and Laurencin. He was just as successful with these artists as he had been with Picasso, Matisse, and Renoir.

After an amazing run of almost ten years, de Hory's forgery spree began to unravel. In 1955 the prestigious Fogg Art Museum at Harvard University bought a faux Matisse from him but then discovered it to be a fake. Later that year, de Hory sold a painting to the Chicago art dealer Joseph Faulkner who realized that it was a forgery. Realizing he had been duped, Faulkner pressed charges that resulted in a federal lawsuit for mail and telephone fraud.

De Hory fled to Mexico City. While he was there, a British homosexual was brutally murdered, and de Hory became a leading suspect in the crime. Although he claimed he had never met the man, de Hory was jailed. When the Mexican police attempted to extort money from him, de Hory hired a lawyer who was a bit of a crook; he charged exorbitant legal fees. Desperate, de Hory paid the lawyer with one of his forgeries and returned to the United States.

Back in the States, de Hory picked up where he left off. To his surprise, several of his own reproductions were listed among the artists' originals as they existed in private collections. When he learned the exorbitant prices these paintings were fetching, de Hory was even more shocked. He realized that the art galleries he had previously dealt with had paid him only a fraction of what his reproductions were actually worth. Ironically, he felt swindled.

Finding himself again short of funds, de Hory resumed his to door-to-door sales at various galleries. But this endeavor took on a great mental and emotional toll. He fell into a deep depression. He was sick of hiding and feeling that he had to conceal so much of his life. It was all getting to be too much for the then fifty-year-old forger. Life had not turned out the way de Hory had expected. He found that continually passing himself off as a fraud disrupted any clear sense of his own identity and caused him much mental deterioration.

This is when he decided to kill himself. In 1968, in his rented Washington, DC flat, de Hory swallowed several handfuls of sleeping pills and waited to die. To his dismay, he was discovered half alive more than a day later and rushed to the hospital, where he recovered. But de Hory's brush with death gave him new hope. He took the fact that he had survived as a sign that he should give life another try. Soon after, he befriended a man who would become his nemesis. The man's name was Fernand Legros, an unscrupulous thief in his own right who aspired to achieve the American Dream by any means necessary. When Legros was introduced to de Hory, he quickly detected de Hory's weak nature and gullibility. Legros set out to use the master forger to his own advantage, and it didn't take long for him to succeed.

Legros convinced de Hory to go into business with him, proposing that he do the dirty work of door-to-door selling for a 40 percent cut while de Hory painted his masterpieces and kept 60 percent. During this time they both were living together in Ibiza, but the police were following them, especially Legros who had a criminal past. Legros felt betrayed by this downward turn in his luck. He became visibly shaken that he was being watched and followed and hunted as a criminal. He then decided to evict de Hory from his house. De Hory had no choice but to flee to Europe. In the meantime the police picked up Legros, who had a history of passing bad checks, and he was sent to jail on these charges.

In 1962 de Hory grew weary eluding the police and decided to return to Ibiza to await his fate. The aging man was apprehended by the police but—oddly enough—not for forgery because there was no proof that he had ever sold a single fraudulent painting in Spain. The charges against him ranged from homosexuality to consorting with known criminals.

De Hory's life took yet another incredible turn. After serving time in jail, he was initially expelled from Spain. Then de Hory returned to his beloved Ibiza only to find that he had become a celebrity. For the first time in his life, he was finally being recognized for his unusual gift for creating masterful forgeries. He appeared on television, collaborated with his pal Clifford Irving in the writing of his biography entitled *Fake!*, and, in 1974, appeared in Orson Welles's documentary, *F for Fake*, which chronicled his life.

Basking in his newfound fame, de Hory began painting again—but this time under his own name. To his delight, he was able to sell many of his own works. These paintings did not sell for as much as his forgeries, but at least he was a legitimate artist earning an honest living who was eager to get on with the rest of his life.

The French authorities, however, continued to pursue him for fraud. Then seventy years old, de Hory couldn't face any possibility of going to jail again for what would surely be a lengthy stay. He decided to take matters into his own hands. On December 1, 1976, de Hory was discovered dead in his home having taken an overdose of sleeping pills. Inevitably, there was some question whether his whole death wasn't a hoax; however, there is not much evidence to support this. De Hory was buried in Ibiza and will forever be noted as one of the island's most illustrious, if not notorious, inhabitants and one of the most talented art forgers the world has ever known.

The Imposter as Exploiter

The fantastic exploits of Irving and de Hory give us an intriguing glimpse into the mind of the imposter. The fact that their deceptions fooled so many for so long is a tribute to not only their chutzpah but to the intensity of their need to cut a swath on the world stage in their struggle to overcome feelings of inferiority and inadequacy. Their self-images were impaired so that what they were able to achieve on their own— abilities that would probably satisfy the needs of most people—were not sufficient to make them feel like winners. Irving was a good writer and de Hory a more-than-competent artist. Both had the demonstrable ability to make a living in their respective artistic endeavors. This, however, was not enough impetus for either man. It was their identification with heroic, important, and powerful figures that spurred them on. It is important to understand how Irving and de Hory were able to integrate their true and false selves and in the process to achieve a degree of inner stability, at least for a reasonable period of time. Obviously, the real self knows that the imposter side is not "really me" or "me as real." Yet far from suffering pangs of anxiety, the imposter feels empowered by his ability to deceive.

The deceptions Irving and de Hory perpetrated can certainly be seen as inspired acts that mimic the actual creative process. Firstly, they must believe intensely in what they are doing to a point where they come to believe in the deception themselves—much like an actor or a novelist. The true artist, however, is aware of the line between reality and fantasy.

With the imposter, however, the boundary between reality and fiction becomes quite shaky.

Irving, for example, knew exactly how to structure a scenario that would convince experienced editors that Hughes did not have to be contacted and that they could reasonably rely on Irving's material. As for de Hory, his job was made easier by the fact that most of the painters whose works he appropriated were dead and could be contacted only through the services of a medium or Ouija board.

Both men played upon the desire of others to provide new or ostensibly lost works by famous artists. Their skill at making these experts into their unwitting collaborators became their true creative act. Perhaps they were before their time—today they might be hailed as performance artists!

I once had a client who embodied the imposter pathology. "Jim" was a young man who had recently graduated from college. He was dating a woman who inspired him to want to do big things for himself. Jim also felt the need to impress her parents, who were quite successful. Although he wanted to marry her, Jim didn't believe he was worthy of either the girl or her family. To resolve this dilemma, he told them that he was starting medical school. Impressed, the parents acquiesced to their marriage plans.

But after the marriage, Jim then had to make his new but deceptive life appear realistic. To do this Jim would leave his apartment every day and come back late in the evening telling his wife about the difficulty of his studies. At dinner with his in-laws, Jim would regale them with his day-to-day activities at medical school, the particulars of which he had gleaned at the public library where he, in reality, spent most of his days. When Jim's wife asked about getting together with some of his fellow students, he would hedge a bit and then tell her that he would approach them. In fact, he started making up stories about some of the women and men he worked with.

Jim was torn. The more he took on the identity of a medical student the better he felt about himself, yet he knew the time would have to come when he would be forced to reveal his deception. Oddly enough, he put this concern out of consciousness and became more and more adroit in developing a believable scenario.

Eventually his wife became suspicious. There were many instances where his stories just didn't add up. But she would put such suspicions aside—the thought that he could be living a completely false life was too fantastic to imagine and would mean their entire relationship was based on a lie.

When the couple socialized, it was invariably with the wife's friends. In their company Jim spun entertaining tales of his life as a medical student. One day Jim's wife was chatting with a woman in a beauty parlor. The subject turned to her husband. The woman asked what medical school he attended and when she told her, the other woman smiled and said that her daughter was also going there. They both remarked on the splendid coincidence and exchanged names.

The following day the wife received a call from her new acquaintance who told her that there must be some mistake: her daughter had told her that there was no such first-year medical school student that bore Jim's name.

That evening, when Jim returned home, an interesting scenario took place.

"So honey," the wife asked, "how was your day?'

"I spent the day in the library studying for tomorrow's exam. Actually, my studies and work are going quite well," Jim replied.

"Have you ever heard of or met a certain Barbara Hirsch?" the wife asked.

"The name doesn't ring a bell," Jim said with a grin on his face, wondering if she was jealous about someone.

"How could you possibly not know of her?" the wife asked. "She would be in your class."

"What was that name again?" Jim asked, trying to buy time.

By now the wife had caught on to his deception.

"Oh, cut it out, will you? This whole damn thing is a sham, isn't it? You've been lying to me all along!"

Jim now realized the whole deception was out in the open. Part of him was relieved, and yet he was terrified by what this revelation would do to their relationship. In fact, it did destroy the marriage. After many anguished conversations, the wife realized that she could no longer live with him; she really didn't know who he was. Her feelings of love for Jim turned into contempt, and she left him and filed for divorce. Following the unraveling of Jim's assumed identity, he faced years of deep depression and a lack of direction as his life lost its meaning.

Assuming the role of the imposter allowed Jim to achieve emotional satisfaction and concrete achievement that he believed would be denied him if he told the truth. The anxiety that imposters feel from living a lie is trumped by a sense of superiority and excitement that comes from the ability to "put one over" on those they do not feel worthy of. Perhaps most importantly, becoming imposters allows them to create a sense of false self-esteem that overcomes feelings of insignificance by creating a fantasy character who has the strength and importance they feel they lack.

Obviously Jim's ruse did not rise to the level of Irving's or de Hory's charades, but all share traits common of the imposter. Most notably, they all felt more authentic when inhabiting their invented personas than when they were their actual selves.

Like all exploiters, Irving and de Hory were shrewd judges of character. They had the ability to discern the needs and desires of those they wanted to deceive. Then they created personas that would satisfy those needs. Like all successful con men, Irving and de Hory bought into the lie themselves, thereby reinforcing its reality.

This type of behavior can be likened to that of a young child who says to himself, *I think it, so it is true*, or, *I think it, so it will happen*. It represents a kind of infantile magical thinking.

Of course, many of us practice magical thinking to varying degrees. A woman, for instance, meets a young man and thinks, *I might fall in love with him*. This idea, however, might prove intimidating—even frightening: What if her feelings are not returned? To lower the emotional stakes, she may tell herself that her flirtation with the man is just a pretense. Now she could easily say to him, "Tom, I love you." It's just a game, after all. The fact that the woman may actually be in love with the man becomes submerged in her subconscious. It is because of this dynamic that so many lies are told in relationships.

With impostors, honesty and integrity assume a low priority. This is necessary in order for them to lose themselves in the character they have created. Who they are is far less important than how they appear to others.

Irving and de Hory must have derived a great deal of pleasure in being able to deceive the bigwigs in the publishing and art worlds. By playing on their insecurities, the imposters charmed these people, inflating their own sense of worth. These bigwigs felt honored to do business with them.

Imposters, then, use a kind of empathy to fashion the nature of their deception. They are able to put themselves into the shoes of the other and accurately gauge what the other most desires.

In the end, however, in overvaluing themselves, imposters devalue their victims who serve only as tools to achieve their own goals. The mark becomes an object of contempt. The public basks in such stories. Just think of the success of such films as *The Sting, Spanish Prisoner,* or *House of Games.*

On an unconscious level, deceit constitutes a type of violence and represents a deliberate assault on the other. Possibly, on a deeper level, maybe the other person has a need to be humiliated to atone for a childhood trauma or to reinforce his low self-esteem. The faux medical student harbored anger and resentment at both his wife and her parents because he felt that they would not accept him as he was. Whether this was true is less important than the fact that he believed it to be true.

Imposters are, by nature, risk-takers. Often they undertake schemes so unlikely to succeed that they are thought either to lack the foresight to see the consequences of their actions, or they are driven by unconscious guilt to engage in activities that will lead to their punishment, or they may even possess a level of delusional narcissism that bestows upon them a feeling of invincibility.

Or as the medical student said to me on one occasion, "Why should I limit myself in how I want to come across to others? The important thing is that I need to appear as successful as I can with no holds barred. At the time, it didn't dawn upon me that I could create such havoc for myself—that I would ruin everything. I hate to say this, but even if I did know how awful it would all come out, I may have acted in a similar fashion."

We all at one time or another harbor dreams that it would be exciting to change identities. Isn't theater all about this—actors taking assumed roles in life and injecting drama into the parts they play? However, at the end of the performance the actor steps back into his regular self. He doesn't walk out of the theater and say that his name is Henry IV or that his name is Picasso.

As alluring as this may appear, there is a line between a fanciful reality and putting on a hoax: a thing called fraud. Imposters are people who cross over this line and then usually pay the price for their deception.

Chapter Six

Don Juans and Gas-Lighters
Men Exploiting Women

You are one of the most famous characters in the history of Western civilization. For the last four centuries, the greatest creative minds in the world have chronicled your exploits, memorializing them in operas, plays, and all manner of literary works. The fascination your name evokes has not faded with time. In fact, you connote a particular sort of man: dashing, handsome, and supremely seductive. Yet, when all is said and done, there is something rather sad about you, a tormented soul with a sleazy facade.

Yes, I am talking to you, Don Juan. Your whole existence, after all, was devoted toward the seduction and abandonment of women. For some deep-seated reason, you are compelled take out your contempt for them at every opportunity. Yet when the thin veneer of your charm is stripped away, you are exposed as a pathetic sort of person, one who cannot love but whose main interests are deception and exploitation. You seduce women and then flee from them. You are driven to repeat this scenario over and over again. And every time you do, the women you have ruined say, "Go to hell!" Oddly enough, in the end, that's exactly what happens: you are literally pulled down into hell.

The age-old legend of Don Juan was first set down in literature in *The Seducer of Seville*. Written in 1630, the play is most commonly attributed to the Spanish monk Tirso de Molina in 1630, according to the *Encyclopedia Britannica*.

The story begins in Naples. Don Juan, the aristocratic son of an old and distinguished Spanish family, seduces Duchess Isabel by pretending, under cover of darkness, to be her fiancé, Duke Octavio. In the ensuing discovery and confusion, Don Juan escapes with the assistance of his uncle, who is the Spanish ambassador to Naples. We learn that Don Juan has seduced other noblewomen back in Spain and that his father has exiled him for his libertine ways. In the course of his flight, Don Juan is shipwrecked, washed ashore at a small Spanish fishing village and nursed back to health by Tisbea, a strong and proud woman who had heretofore been contemptuous of love. Don Juan overcomes her reticence with sweet words and claims of everlasting love. "I am dying for you," he tells her. Don Juan then beds her and afterward flees after burning down Tisbea's hut.

Don Juan then returns to his native city of Seville. His faithful servant, Leporello, is both frightened and fascinated by his master's actions. He continually urges Don Juan to reform his wicked ways in order to escape death, damnation, and the torments of hell. Don Juan laughs scornfully at such fears: "I have a long time left to worry about that!"

By chance, an invitation from Dona Ana, daughter of the commendatore of the military order of Calatrava, to her beloved Marquis de la Mota falls into Don Juan's hands. Disguising himself as the Marquis (who is his friend) while sending him to another part of the city, Don Juan gains admittance to Dona Ana's rooms and seduces her. When Dona Ana discovers his real identity and realizes that she has been tricked, she screams for help. Her father rushes in to avenge both his daughter's dishonor and his own disgrace; however, Don Juan kills him and escapes again.

Don Juan now exults in his reputation as "the great deceiver of women; the Trickster of Spain." Even more than seduction, he says that "the greatest pleasure is to trick women and leave them dishonored." Again, his servant warns him of his evil ways. Even Don Juan's father begs him to change. But the libertine continues to scoff at their warnings. "Plenty of time for that later," Don Juan crows.

Fleeing from justice after the murder of Dona Ana's father, Don Juan enters a village wedding feast. Setting his sights on the bride, he uses his arsenal of promises and ruses, seducing the virgin bride only hours after the ceremony—and again he flees.

Returning to Seville in disguise, Don Juan, accompanied by his servant, enters a church. They see a stone statue over the vault of the commendatore who Don Juan had so recently killed. The inscription of the base calls for vengeance. Defiant, Don Juan pulls the beard of the statue and invites the effigy to dinner at his house.

That night the statue, which has come to life, appears at the door. Don Juan is clearly surprised and, for the first time, uneasy, but he welcomes his visitor. The statue then invites Don Juan to supper at his tomb on the next night. Don Juan accepts with a show of bravado: "Were you hell itself, I would dare to give my hand."

When Don Juan appears at the tomb, the statue of the commendatore says, "For what you have you done, you must pay!" He then grips Don Juan's hand to drag him down into the fiery tortures of hell. Don Juan resists, at first placing the blame for the seduction on Dona Ana on someone else. When that doesn't work, he tries to repent by calling for a priest. "Your resolve is too late," replies the statue. With that, Don Juan dies, and the tomb sinks with him into hell.

This play established the basic plot elements used by those who later took up the story: Don Juan tricks and seduces a series of women; Don Juan challenges the statue of a man whom he killed in the course of his seductions, a challenge that leads ultimately to his punishment.

The themes of seduction, deception, and murder are common to the types of exploiters who hone their skills on women. In psychology, both the terms "Don Juan-ism" and "Don Juan-esque" are used to denote a type of man who exploits women by lying and deceiving them. Studies suggest that the outward personality of a Don Juan is in direct opposition to their inner self. The seemingly macho guy with a high testosterone level is likely to be sexually immature and weak in psyche and physique. His over-the-top behavior masks an indecisive masculinity: indecisive because much of his behavior can be traced back to his conflicts with the irreplaceable mother. So the man needs to replace the women again and again.

As for the men he cuckolds and even kills, they represent the unconquerable mortal enemy, the father. This would follow the Oedipal theme in psychology. Don Juan's initial taunt to the statue can be seen as the ultimate challenge to the father's potency. He pulls the statue's beard, possibly representing his penis, a supreme insult, symbolically challenging the surrogate father's power. Don Juan also competes with sexual rivals of his own age—his friend the Marquis de la Mota and the village bridegroom, for example. His rivals, in fact, are almost as important as the women. He never has separated from his parental conflicts—he just carries them forward into adulthood where he acts them out.

More striking still underneath it all is the Don Juan's brutality toward women. As soon as he has seduced them, he flees or causes them harm, presumably in a futile attempt to work out his childhood ambivalence with his mother. He burns down Tisbea's hut to get back at her because she could not satisfy his quest for gratification. The pleasure he derives from the conquest and deception of women is much more intense than the sex act itself.

A Don Juan-esque man is driven to find his mother in all women. His striving for sexual satisfaction is an attempt to gain a kind of self-fulfillment, a gratification of some unconscious fantasy of conquering the mother. But this quest is impossible to gratify him, and he then becomes frustrated in failing to achieve it. The failure to ultimately find satisfaction results in his ensuing hostility toward women. He is not interested in the actual women he attempts to seduce; rather, his driven sexual activity is primarily designed to overcome an inner feeling of inferiority by proving to himself how successful he is. In this sense, the women are only used as pawns in his attempt to overcome his feelings of inadequacy. After seducing a woman, Don Juan loses interest in her because she too has failed to raise his self-esteem. His narcissistic personality requires proof of his ability to excite women; but once he has done that, his doubts about his potency resurface. Thus, he is forced to continually repeat this behavior, much like the gambler who hopes to hit it big and then is forced to gamble over and over again in spite of the losses.

Don Juan's sexual pathology is an obsession that masks a striving for power or prestige. Actually, he is riddled with such fear that underneath it all he really isn't so potent after all. Remember, for the infant child, the mother is the original and most complete source of satisfaction. In the normal maturing process, the child rejects the mother and finds pleasure in other, more appropriate women. Giving up the mother is never easy, but staying attached to her will hinder the growth of the adult male. When the attachment to the mother is too strong, it serves to cast all other women as inevitable disappointments. They are never seen as real women for who they are but represent a fantasy of how they can satisfy the male's neurotic cravings.

So we can see that Don Juan takes the route of a man who is overly involved with his mother's early image. He is not able to get her and thereby develops this frustration and hostility. He continues to have an insatiable longing for some total pleasure of fusion with the mother. He cannot simply reject women, for he needs them to work out this classic dilemma, hoping that they will bring him the pleasure of the mother that he craves. He is driven in this exaggerated male striving for sexual control, power, and prestige.

All boys will experience the mother at some time in their lives as a source of frustration and pleasure, yet not all boys grow up to become Don Juans. Most use other mechanisms to handle their frustrations, ones that enable them to pursue mature, mutually rewarding relationships. For the Don Juans, frustration and pleasure must be combined in some special way that produces insatiable longing together with aggressive rage. For them, women will always be alluring and loving but also faithless and treacherous. A Don Juan approaches women with his affectionate seduction, but then he must demean them. That is why his aim in life is riddled with the need to exploit women.

In short, the Don Juan-esque man seeks to unite with the mother through seducing a series of women, yet he fears intimacy, which is tied to worries that could cause his destruction, as represented in the play by Don Juan's unwilling descent into hell. He cannot separate his attraction and anger toward women because they have been complexly bound together by virtue of his dysfunctional view of the mother. Symbols of this complex combination—the ocean, the statue, and the tomb—represent the swallowing up of the male. Don Juan's behavior—deprecation of women, bragging, insolence, and violence—are means to gain power to control his chaotic and confused sources of pain and pleasure. Underneath it all lies a rather pathetic man whose infantile conflict cannot be resolved.

In Mozart's opera *Don Giovanni*, the servant recites the catalogue of "beauties my master has loved": "In Italy, six hundred and forty; In German, two hundred thirty-one; One hundred in France, ninety-one in Turkey; but in Spain there are already a thousand and three...Provided she wears a skirt, you know what he does..." (Act 1, Scene 2).

In the original play, Don Juan carries out two of his four seductions by means of disguise, taking advantage of the darkness to conceal his true identity and instead appearing as the man with whom the woman is in love: Don Octavio in the case of Isabel and the Marquis de la Mota with Dona Ana. In later versions of the legend, Don Juan carries this attempt at disguise even further: he changes costumes with his servant, for instance, and takes on other disguises. It is obviously a useful tactic for seduction whether the women are genuinely deceived about his identity or are using his ruses as an excuse for willing participation.

Moreover, Don Juan conceals his identity only when seducing women of noble or aristocratic rank and only when the seduction occurs in a palace or a noble house. This environment represents the true threat to his behavior because he is so impressed by the power of its position.

But Don Juan does more than just disguise himself in order to seduce. When Isabel first discovers the trickery and asks, "Who are you?" He replies, "I am a man without a name." The King of Naples rushes in and asks, "Who's there?" Don Juan replies, "A man and a woman"—two sexes, two nameless individuals—biological forces without title or status. It is as though Don Juan feels that he has no true identity and so assumes whatever name, costume, and background is required to carry through his plots.

Don Juan seems to be in control of everyone and everything: the women he seduces, his servants, and those who would reprimand and punish him. He arranges and maneuvers every situation so that he can act upon it as he desires. "Who can confine Don Juan, who is himself unconfined?" asks one servant. Both sexually and socially, Don Juan strives to avoid being confined or ensnared in the demands and arrangements of other people.

In this way, Don Juan lives out the fantasy of many men, a career of glorious conquest, until his arrogant behavior leads to his destruction. His legend is an imaginative treatise on the nature of power in the form of sexual conquest arising from the fear of a powerful and binding mother.

The Don Juan pathology can be seen in a spectrum of abusive relationships. It is a narcissistic disorder. Narcissism is a term that has been bantered around and has come to mean different things. The term *normal narcissism* denotes aspects of feelings that non-pathological people have toward themselves: a sense of their own self-esteem, concern for their own physical and mental states, and a sense of their legitimate rights. Unhealthy narcissists exhibit exaggerated feelings of entitlement: they have an obsessive need to be admired. It is their belief that they deserve everything and have to denigrate others whom they secretly envy. Often they feel bored and empty. The Don Juan pontificates rather than speaks. He is careless and unemphathic of others and of their feelings. In fact, others serve as only as an audience whose existence serves to admire and mirror his grandiosity.

The saddest symptom of an unhealthy narcissist is an incapacity to love. There is a decided lack of empathy on the narcissist's part and a difficulty in feeling gratitude and remorse. In fact, both apologizing and expressing gratitude implies being able to feel concern for another person—recognizing one's own error when one apologizes and one's own need when one says thank you. The narcissist is not able to recognize his own needs or his own mistakes, because it would be too painful; he doesn't have what it takes to deepen his feeling.

The erotic behavior of Don Juan seems to show complete freedom from sexual taboos. But his promiscuity really demonstrates his submission to these prohibitions in that he is unable to obtain any deep pleasure from his conquests. Don Juan, persecuted by his internalized parents, must always flee from the woman he has conquered to search for another woman. Part of this purpose is to punish the women because they shall suffer for having sought their personal genital fulfillment.

In truth, Don Juan is depraved and perverted. His main interest in life is to destroy the female. The pervert's object is to control others, to deny their autonomy. The pervert never questions his own behavior: since he cannot experience conflict within himself, he must expel it, transfer it to someone else. The pervert derives pleasure in making others suffer. He creates an atmosphere of distress and fear. He is also a cynic, believing and acting as if there is nothing good, noble, or sacred in the world, as if everyone and everything deserves the same measure of contempt.

As we can see in the next example, the pervert cannot act on his own; he needs another person, someone he can use for his own purposes to exploit and destroy. In this sense, perversion is understood as it functions within a relationship, as the pervert derives pleasure from his ability to manipulate and subjugate.

The Gas-Lighter

The term "gas-lighting" derives from the 1940 film *Gaslight,* which was adapted from the stage play *Angel Street. Gaslight* is the story of a man, played by the actor Charles Boyer, who marries a woman, played by Ingrid Bergman, and tries to drive her insane as part of a plot to retrieve jewels hidden in the house in which the couple is living.

Twenty years earlier, an old woman was murdered in that house for those very jewels, but they were never found. As the plot develops, the audience discovers that it was the husband, Boyer, who killed the old woman and is now trying to have his wife committed so he can get her out of the way and find the jewels he was unable to locate at the time of his crime.

In *Gaslight* one of the ways the husband tries to pry loose the wife's grip on reality is by telling her she is delusional when she notices the gaslight in the house dimming, something that he is doing deliberately and hence the coining of the term "gas-lighting."

Throughout the film, the wife tries to understand what is happening to her as the husband attempts to undermine the validity of her perception. What is happening is that the husband perpetrates these distortions and then denies that anything of the sort is going on. He even claims that he is the victim. The husband's actions are those of a psychological terrorist.

In a 1981 paper dealing with gas-lighting, psychiatrist Victor Calef and psychoanalyst Edward M. Weinsheld describe a case that brings further clarity and understanding to this kind of person. The patient, a young woman, is married to a man she describes as handsome and successful, forceful, articulate, and quietly domineering. The husband at first seemed to her to be solid and normal—in many ways the epitome of the all-American boy. The wife was a quiet, retiring, but intelligent woman. Although she had done extremely well at college, she appeared to be content to submerge her own interests and talents to her husband's needs and career.

The couple started a family, and as the years went on, the wife and the children began to exhibit neurotic and phobic behaviors. Both husband and wife agreed that it was her mental problems that were responsible for the children's difficulties—that she was a disturbed, illogical woman whose actions appeared to verge on the psychotic. To resolve the situation, the couple went into therapy. For a long time, the nature of their difficulties remained unclear to their respective therapists.

Here is an example of the family dynamic, one that creates enormous tension in the family. The husband is speeding through the city streets at fifty or more miles per hour with his wife and children. The husband drives calmly with an air of nonchalance. He does, however, repeatedly warn his wife and children to keep an eye out for the police.

His family becomes increasingly fearful and begs the husband/father to slow down. He demeans them for their fears. He is content that he is behaving normally and believes his wife and children to be overly emotional and irrational. Fortunately, no catastrophe occurs.

Over the years, the marriage continued with relatively little change, especially in regard to this conflicted relationship of the husband and wife. He was coolly tolerant of her illness, but at the same time he made it clear that he was displeased and aggrieved having to put up with an unbalanced spouse.

Eventually the wife and children sought therapy, and in doing so, their relationship to the husband/father changed, first subtly and then more strikingly. The wife began to recognize her husband's domineering behavior and then attempted to develop a life of her own, becoming active in community affairs and, for the first time, speaking up in social situations. At first her husband seemed pleased, but after a while he became annoyed and openly disparaging of his wife's newfound autonomy. When no one responded to his criticisms and to attempts to undermine the improvement in the rest of the family, the husband/father began to withdraw, became despondent, and finally developed a series of psychosomatic conditions. As his mental state deteriorated, the husband too exhibited a series of bizarre actions that disrupted his professional life. Finally, his marriage dissolved and the couple divorced. Afterward, the husband married a much younger woman who seemed content to accept the role that the previous wife had rejected. The woman remarried, and both she and the children continued to develop socially and academically.

This case presents a clear picture of the dynamic of gas-lighting where the exploiter attempts to inflict damage and undermine the other person's understanding of reality. The other person then is treated as a victim where he or she becomes increasingly uncertain and confused regarding his or her assessment of internal and external perceptions. The victimizer's control of his or her prey enables the victim to feel more normal and in control.

The experience of the victim is more complex. Some individuals will respond to the victimizer with a mature, non-conflicted reply, others with angry rejection, and still others with what appears on the surface to be a docile, uncritical acceptance. Not all individuals will react in the same fashion to the gas-lighter's attempt. If the victimizer can tap into and play upon his or her victim's internal conflict involving guilt or shame, the chances of being successful are enhanced considerably.

But once the victim breaks free of the gas-lighter's control, the victimizer's perception of himself or herself begins to crumble, based as it was on his or her ability to exert complete control over the significant others in his or her life.

Psychological Manipulation

The gas-lighter manipulates his or her victims in a much different manner than other exploiters. Gas-lighters attempt to alter the perception or behavior of others through underhanded, deceptive, or even abusive tactics. They attempt to impose devious and underhanded methods of influencing the other person. At times the attempt may not be considered as abusive or deceptive, while other kinds of manipulation aim to severely cripple the other person.

Looking at the evil parts of this, we can turn to brainwashing. The Maoist regime in China aimed to transform individuals with a reactionary imperialist mindset into "right-thinking" members of the new Chinese social system. To this end the regime developed techniques that would break down the psychic integrity of the individual with regard to information processing, information retained in the mind, and individual values. They had many techniques at their disposal. These techniques usually attempted to dehumanize the individuals by keeping them in filth, sleep deprivation, partial sensory deprivation, psychological harassment, inculcation of guilt, and group social pressure.

In fact, there was a film, *The Manchurian Candidate*, that brought the issue of mind control to its ultimate evil intent. Raymond Shaw returns from the Korean War, a superhero and holder of the Congressional Medal of Honor, but some in his platoon question what Shaw actually did to deserve the medal. They were all prisoners of war and Marco, a fellow soldier, began to have recurring nightmares about Korea and decides to investigate his awful dreams more thoroughly. Piece by piece, he is able to put the story together. It turns out that the entire platoon was captured by North Koreans and brainwashed to think that Shaw was a hero when, in truth, he had been programmed to be a killer. But who is he to kill? Upon his return from service, Shaw leaves his overly protective mother and her husband, a right-wing senator. Shaw then goes to work as a journalist, but when his control, a foreign element, contacts him with the code that is implanted in his brain, he kills without mercy or memory; a liberal columnist-publisher is his first victim. Shaw, now married, is next sent to kill his own wife and his father-in-law, a liberal senator. Marco discovers the truth in time, and the plot reveals that Shaw's controller is his mother, the top Communist spy in the United States. She orders her robot-like son to kill the presidential nominee; her husband who is the vice-presidential running mate will then take control of the White House. However, in the end, Marco is able to foil the plot in a very moving and exciting finish.

Obviously, there are mind-control strategies that are not as abusive or vicious as in *The Manchurian Candidate*. On this continuum there are even attempts that are more benign and in some cases actually a bit funny. Psychological games then vary widely in degrees of pleasantness. Eric Berne wrote a book in 1966 called *Games People Play*. The games he was referring to were based on ulterior transactions, and all contained some element of exploitation.

We all need some kind of appreciation from others so that even if relationships are negative that appreciation could be considered to be better than none at all. The need for intimacy is also why people engage in games—games become substitutes for genuine contact. These games have ulterior motives, and therefore, they are played to satisfy some hidden motive and always involve a payoff. Most of time we are not aware we are playing games; this is just a normal part of social interaction. Games then can be seen much like playing poker, in which one's real motivation is hidden as part of the strategy to achieve the payoff—to win money. When we move this idea to the work environment, the payoff may be achieving the deal; people speak of being in the real estate game or the insurance game. A popular book some time ago was called *Money Game*.

In his book Berne highlights many different kinds of games that people play. The most common games are played between spouses, in which one partner complains that the other is an obstacle to doing what he or she really wants to do in life. The suggestion here is that most people unconsciously choose spouses because they want certain limits placed upon them. He gives an example of a woman who seemed desperate to learn to dance. The problem was that her husband hated going out, so her social life was restricted. In desperation she enrolled in dancing classes but found that she was terribly afraid of dancing in public and dropped out. In this case, Berne points out that what we blame the other partner for is more often revealed as an issue within ourselves.

Playing "if it weren't for you" allows us to divest ourselves of responsibility for facing our fears or shortcomings.

The game begins when a person states a problem in his or her life and another person responds by offering constructive suggestions on how to solve it. The subject says "yes, but…" and proceeds to find issue with the solutions. If he or she were acting as the adult he or she would examine and probably work for a solution (an Adult stance), but this is not the purpose of the exchange. Its underlying purpose is to allow the subject to gain sympathy from others in their inadequacy to meet the situation (Child mode). This pushes the problem-solvers to act as a kind of parent. It can be seen as a subtle kind of exploitation but one that is not that abusive.

For most, the games, if we play them at all, are factors that we inherit from childhood and continue to let roll. They serve to absolve us of the need to really confront unresolved psychological issues. People who continually affirm that the reason they can't do something is because they had a hard and difficult childhood use this reason as a built-in excuse. They then look for another person to confirm this, thereby absolving them of their real fear of taking action. Berne advises that if you play too many 'bad' games for too long, they become self-destructive. The more games you play, the more you expect others to play them too; a relentless game-player can end up a psychotic who reads too much of his or her own motivations and biases into others' behavior.

Going back to gas-lighting, it would seem difficult to consider these activities as games. Boyer in the film aimed not to kill his wife but to certainly drive her crazy. In this way, his goal was to destroy her mind while all along making her feel as if he were this nurturing and caring individual. The next case used his family to work out his aggressive and destructive needs. Once separated from them he had no victims to project this hostility and so became depressed and despairing.

On a more humorous note, a book by Stephen Potter in 1952 was titled *The Theory And Practice Of Gamesmanship Or The Art of Winning Games Without Actually Cheating*. In this context, the term refers to a satiric course in the gambits required for the systematic and conscious practice of "creative intimidation," making one's associates feel inferior and thereby gaining the status of being "one up" on them.

The satire of Potter's self-help guide manipulates traditional stuffy British conventions for the gamester, all life being a game where one must understand that *if you're not one up, you're one down*. Potter's unprincipled principles apply to almost any possession, experience, or situation, serving maximum underserved rewards and discomforting the opposition. The aim is to undermine the credibility of the other person, at times even to place the other person in a halo of an inferior standing among his or her colleagues.

All this is quite different from the Don Juans and gas-lighters who project their rage and fear onto women and take satisfaction in their suffering. Both types are incapable of empathy and cannot accept women as independent whole beings. Possibly, this makes them feel strong in that it allows them to deny feelings of infantile terror and dependency. Control of the women represents revenge on the perceived weakness of the mother and of women in general.

But the women's role in this dynamic must also be examined. In all cases, there is collusion between the partners. The woman must get something from the maltreatment. She may think that if she were a better person the relationship would improve. She tries to modify her behavior but to no avail. Her partner's devaluation and criticism are always at the ready, but while he is very clear in maintaining that she is in the wrong, he is unclear when it comes to making a pronouncement as to what she should do to improve things.

Why do women submit to maltreatment? Possibly, like the females of other animal species, women use all their resources to preserve the nest. In the perverse relationship, the woman finds herself thinking that if her husband is maltreating her it means that she is guilty. It is, to be sure, a perverse logic, but a logic that lends order to the world. In many cases this sense of order—even gained at such a painful price—is preferable to the chaos and confusion that would result if she did not take all the blame upon herself. If the man becomes more irrational and incomprehensible, the woman compensates by devoting her energies to developing strategies to cope with the situation. In doing so she becomes more bound up in the relationship, isolating herself from friends and family who might be able to rectify the warped self-image that she and her victimizer have, however subconsciously, collaborated to create.

It is interesting to contemplate that the Don Juan and the gas-lighter both have a desperate need for the women they think so little of. Without them, they would be left to deal with their underlying conflicts alone—the very thing they cannot tolerate.

Chapter Seven

Manic Greed: The Thrill of Money, Power, and Breaking Boundaries Jack Abramoff and Michael Milken

Let's envision the following scenario. A sleek, newly built luxury liner was cutting through the waters of the Mediterranean Sea. It was a bright April evening and aboard were some of the richest, most successful, and influential group of people. The ship featured the finest cuisine, and of course, all of the amenities were crafted with exquisite detail. Being a passenger on this liner meant in everyday language that you have made it in life—that you have arrived at the top of your game and now you are taking from society all the accoutrements of the good life.

It was now after dinner and some of the passengers had gone into the intimate cocktail lounge for a nightcap and where they would be serenaded by a sophisticated pianist who treated the people to the best of Cole Porter and Rogers and Hart. It was here off to the corner of the room that two men found themselves in close proximity. There was a spark and an expression of exuberance in each of their faces; they loved themselves and the world around them. It was a love affair made in heaven. They noticed the other, nodded their heads, and then were drawn into conversation as if they had rediscovered a long-lost relative. They introduced themselves to each other.

Extending his hand, "Jack Abramoff."

"Glad to make your acquaintance," replied Michael Milken.

Soon afterward they got to the usual social questions that enable people to know whether there is enough interest to go further in searching the other out.

Abramoff spoke first. "I'm a lobbyist in Washington DC. In fact, I started in this business while I was still in college. It gives me the chance to become friends with some of the most important political figures. I even have my own restaurant where I can entertain some of the important people that I come into contact with."

He smiled and went on talking. "Now I am engaged in an important project with a number of Indian tribes who are seeking gambling concessions, and since I know almost everyone," he chuckled, "they came to me, and after my introduction to them about who I am, they hired me for the job. They do have quite a lot of money, and we both know, or I believe we both know, that money talks in this town. And what about you?"

Milken studied the man opposite him for a moment and then launched into a presentation of himself.

"Actually, I deal in the financial business of providing bonds to institutions who want to expand or take over other institutions. I also know the movers and the shakers in the financial world. Some people refer to my bonds as junk bonds, meaning they may not have high ratings but they deliver what is promised to my customers. You can't believe the frantic pace of my business; literally, I don't have a minute to myself. If my wife did not give me an ultimatum about this trip, I could have gone on working. I work for Drexel Burnham, and we are raking in the money."

Abramoff shook his head and now wanted to forge a closer bond with this high roller.

"So what do you think moves us in these directions? You in finance and me in pushing my influence."

"What's your take on it?" questioned Milken.

"My hunch is that we are addicted to the excitement and the action that we experience each day. That's what I think."

Milken now shook his head to affirm what he had just heard. "Yes, I think you are right. When the money starts to roll in I feel like Superman who can fly over high buildings. I just can't tell you the thrill of the whole thing, but I think you know quite well what I am talking about. You can feel it in your skin, your voice, your driveness.

We have another five days so we have a chance to get to know each other better."

"Let's stay in touch." There was such a rich pleasure extending in their faces. Their energy levels locked forces and formed a keen attachment. They shook hands and both agreed that's what they wanted to do—get to know each other better and share in this mutual excitement.

Abramoff and his Lobbying Enterprise

On November 6, 2011, Jack Abramoff was hosting a coming-out party. He was in the process of rolling out his rehabilitative media campaign. There were friends and colleagues. Among them were his lawyer, his publicist, his literary agent, and a wealthy investor. They were going to watch Jack on *60 Minutes*, with popcorn, potato chips, and seltzer; a kosher sushi dinner waited in the main room—quite an affair considering he had just gotten out of prison.

He was for hire for speaking engagements and came after serving three and a half years for crimes that included corrupting members of Congress with illegal golf trips to Scotland as well as bilking Indian tribes out of lots of dough. He now owed more than $40 million to these tribes, but his mind was riveted to the many projects he had in mind. The energy and drive that propelled him into his lobbying activities had now been turned into a much different use of himself. He felt that he could turn the problems from his past into becoming a successful motivational speaker who could educate his listeners on how to keep their lives on the straight and moral path. This guy would always make it, and the people in the room felt he was sincere and persuasive—the ingredients of a sure winner.

On January 3, 2006, Abramoff pled guilty to three felony counts—conspiracy, fraud, and tax evasion—involving charges stemming from his lobbying activities in Washington on behalf of Native American tribes. Abramoff and other defendants had to make restitution of at least $25 million defrauded from clients, most notably the Native American tribes. Further, he owed the Internal Revenue Service $1.7 million as a result of his guilty plea to the tax-evasion charge. As part of the deal with the Justice Department, Abramoff, who at the time was forty-seven years old with a wife and five children, agreed to cooperate with a widening federal probe into corruption of government officials.

The disgraced lobbyist, whose career was characterized by extraordinary risk-taking, ideological zealotry, and outsized greed, had been under federal scrutiny for almost two years. Previously, Michael Scanlon, who had been a covert lobbying partner of Abramoff's in his American Indian casino work, pleaded guilty to fraud and conspiracy charges.

On January 4, 2006, cohorts of Abramoff pleaded guilty in Miami to separate charges of wire fraud. This involved a fraudulent $23 million wire transfer that Abramoff and a business associate, Adam Kidan, used in 2000 as proof of their down payment to swindle $60 million from lenders for their short-lived acquisition of Florida-based SunCruz Casino. Kidan was sentenced to five years and ten months by a Florida judge for his crimes.

Numerous others were caught up in the web of conspiracy. Tony Rudy, an aide to former House Majority Leader Tom DeLay of Texas, pleaded guilty to a one-count conspiracy charge. Rudy acknowledged that he did legislative favors for Abramoff in exchange for gifts and money—including numerous meals, luxury trips, and tens of thousands of dollars—while he worked in DeLay's office. Others pleaded guilty to conspiracy charges, notably Representative Bob Ney of Ohio who was chairman of the House Administration Committee, which oversaw lobbying, federal elections, and operations of the House of Representatives.

In addition, DeLay had taken three trips to such far-flung locales as Scotland, Moscow, and the Northern Mariana Islands in the Pacific. The political fallout was enormous. Dozens of politicos—Republican and Democrat—scrambled to return or donate to charity campaign contributions from several tribes that Abramoff represented and from the lobbyist himself to avoid being tarred by accusations of political corruption in the upcoming elections. Included in this web of fraud were conservative lobbyists Grover Norquist, the leader of an influential tax-reform group, and Ralph Reed, former head of the Christian Coalition. Both had been Abramoff's political allies for almost a quarter century and benefitted financially from Abramoff's Indian casino work.

At the close of his court appearance in Washington, a grim-looking Abramoff made a brief statement: "All of my remaining days, I will feel tremendous sadness and regret for my conduct and for what I have done," he said, speaking in a subdued voice. "I only hope I can merit forgiveness from the Almighty and from those who I have wronged or caused to suffer" (Stone 2006).

Abramoff's career in Washington was characterized by a vaunting ambition and manic drive. He told a magazine reporter that despite his mistakes and errors of judgment—which he attributed largely to his style of operating at breakneck speed—"I was the best thing [the Indians] had going." He added, "You're really no one in this town, unless you have met me."

Abramoff's sad story tells a tale of political corruption that spawned an extraordinary powerful influence machine that his clients bankrolled. The corruption schemes Abramoff fostered highlight the often hidden ways in which campaign cash and lobbying favors exert influence over decision making in Washington.

At an earlier time, Abramoff was hailed as a savior to the Tigua Indians of Texas, a tribe with thirteen hundred members that had been in the El Paso area since 1680. However, the tribe fell on hard times in 2002 when a Texas court ordered that a highly profitable casino that it had been running since 1993 be shuttered. It was then that Abramoff approached the tribe saying that he could help reopen their casino.

It was a welcome offer. The Tiguas had no political clout, and the millions of dollars their enterprise generated was vital to the tribe's fiscal well-being. The money from the casino had funded such projects as a $20 million state-of-the-art wellness center that offered everything from a diabetes prevention and treatment program to karate classes for children to a modern Olympic-size swimming pool and other recreational facilities. During the years when the casino was operating, the tribe's unemployment rate, which had previously hovered around 50 percent, was close to zero, and the tribe was able to pay each of its members between $8,000 and $15,000 as well as provide health insurance to many. Without the resources from the casino, the tribe would be in dire straits.

Abramoff's résumé was more than enough to impress anyone—it read like a Who's Who of the GOP power elite. At that time, he was a hot item and had received extensive and favorable press coverage. Abramoff had been lionized in front-page stories in *The New York Times* and *The Wall Street Journal*. The articles highlighted his fund-raising efforts for Republicans, particularly mentioning DeLay, who was referred to as one of Abramoff's closest and dearest friends.

A stocky, well-built man in his early forties who had once been a star weight lifter in Beverly Hills High School, Abramoff possessed a smooth, polished style. He, together with Michael Scanlon, a former spokesman for DeLay who turned into a public relations and grassroots consultant, had flown to El Paso in a privately chartered Gulfstream II jet. They made their entrance as if they owned the world, sharply dressed and armed with a finely honed sales pitch. They told the Tigua tribe that they wielded enormous power in Congress and could get many of its members to champion the Tiguas' cause.

The elders listened raptly as Abramoff laid out his plans for success. He offered to do pro bono work for the Tiguas, telling the tribal chiefs that the casino's closing was outrageous. While he would work pro bono, his colleague Scanlon would have to be paid as a consultant. Abramoff told them that he already found some members of Congress who would correct the injustice citing "a couple of senators willing to ram this through" (Stone). There would be, he stressed, a need for absolute secrecy in order for the initiative to succeed.

Carlos Hisa, the head of the tribal council, said that when he looked up Abramoff on the Internet he was totally impressed: his credentials were impeccable. The tribe realized immediately that Abramoff was the man to save the day. Abramoff then informed them that $300,000 donations to key legislators and committees had to be made quickly. The checks should be made out to Abramoff who would then distribute them. The tribe agreed.

In a matter of days, Abramoff told the tribe that he already had a commitment from a little-known but influential House Republican, Bob Ney of Ohio, chairman of the House Administration Committee, who would attach a measure to an election reform bill that would permit the casino to reopen. Later, he instructed the tribe to donate some $32,000 to Ney's campaign committee and a newly created political action committee, which the Tiguas quickly did. And for good measure, Abramoff asked the Tiguas to chip in $50,000 to underwrite a golf junket to Scotland for Ney and two of his staff that August.

The tribe then reached out to another small Texas tribe, the Alabama-Coushatta, which might also benefit from the proposed legislation because they too had a casino project that was in jeopardy. The Tigua proposed that the Coushatta chip in some of the money they were paying Abramoff. The Alabama-Coushatta listened to the proposal and agreed to finance the golf junket. The tribe was instructed to send the money to an obscure Abramoff-run charity in Washington called the 'Capital Athletic Foundation,' which would in turn pay for the trip and book it as an educational mission in order to avoid public disclosure about its actual funding sources.

In keeping with Abramoff's passion for extravagance, the trip ran to $130,000. Abramoff added a few more people to his payroll, such as

Ralph Reed and Neil Volz, former chief of staff for Bob Ney. The entourage flew to St. Andrews on a rented Gulfstream II jet and enjoyed spacious $400-a-night rooms at the Old Course Hotel and elegant dining in Edinburgh. For good measure, there was also a two-day stopover at the expensive Mandarin Oriental Hyde Park Hotel in London on the way home.

Days later, Hisa and his advisor Marc Schwartz traveled to Washington where they met with Ney and Abramoff in the congressman's office for almost ninety minutes and received assurances of his support for their cause. Afterward, Abramoff continued to impress the tribe with his Washington clout. He went as far as to tell them that President Bush had contacted him and asked him to help find individuals to place in certain offices.

Unfortunately for the Tiguas, the legislation that Ney assured the tribe he would push through never became law. Ney backed out after the influential Democratic congressman Christopher Dodd denied he would support the bill even though Abramoff had assured Ney of Dodd's backing. The failure of the bill was just the start of the tribe's ordeal with Abramoff. They learned that despite Abramoff's pledge that he would initially work pro bono for the tribe, he had in fact split most of the $4.2 million they had paid Scanlon.

Additionally, Hisa and the tribe subsequently discovered that Abramoff and Scanlon, before they approached the Tiguas, had actually been engaged in a lobbying drive whose aim was to shut down the very same 'Speaking Rock' casino they were now pressing to reopen. The effort had been financed by another casino-owning tribe, *Coushatta Tribe* of *Louisiana*. Although the Tiguas were located almost eight hundred miles away, Abramoff had convinced the Louisiana Coushattas that both the Tiguas and the Alabama-Coushattas, who were nearer the Louisiana border, posed serious threats to its revenues.

These revelations sent Abramoff into a frenzy. Just days before the Tiguas' casino was to close, he fired off an e-mail to Reed saying, "I wish those moronic Tiguas were smarter in their political contributions. I'd love us to get our mitts on that moolah. Oh well stupid people get wiped out" (Stone). While Abramoff and Scanlon were making plans for their visit to El Paso, Abramoff wrote to Scanlon, "Fire up the jet baby we're going to El Paso!!" Scanlon simply responded, "I want all their money." Abramoff assented, "Yawzah."

Hisa, of course, regretted the whole venture with Abramoff and was haunted by the fact that he asked another tribe to make such a large donation to help Ney take his golf junket. "I feel like I did what Abramoff did to us," he said (Stone).

What happened to the Tiguas was actually just a fragment of a much wider pattern of fraud that Abramoff and Scanlon perpetrated on several tribes flush with casino revenue. The tribes that hired the two lobbyists were among the wealthiest in the country thanks to their casino revenues, which in some cases brought in $300 million or more annually. In the 2000s, Abramoff made millions of dollars for himself and kept the GOP coffers brimming.

The Indian gaming industry was also growing at a rapid pace: by the end of 2005, Indian casinos were a $20-billion-a-year industry and represented the fastest-growing segment of the nation's gambling enterprises.

However, in spite of their newfound wealth, the tribes were relatively unsophisticated when it came to the Beltway politics. They were ripe pickings for someone with Abramoff's exploitive personality. He knew they had the money, and he knew how to lure them into this trap. The *Saginaw Chippewa Indian Tribe* of Michigan spent almost $14 million to hire Scanlon and, like the Tiguas, had no knowledge that he had a secret kickback deal with Abramoff.

The bitter and very costly experiences that the Tiguas, the Saginaw Chippewas, and several other tribes had with Abramoff and Scanlon helped lift the lid on a giant influence-peddling scandal. Ultimately, it was revealed that six tribes paid Abramoff and Scanlon the extraordinary sum of $82 million over three years for their lobbying and PR help.

The ensuing Senate hearings uncovered a mountain of evidence, including a treasure trove of e-mail traffic between Abramoff, Scanlon, and other lobbyists that detailed the often bizarre and complex cons they used to manipulate tribes into paying them such large fees. They had an insatiable appetite for more deals and more money. On December 7, 2002, Abramoff e-mailed Scanlon: "We really need mo money...We are missing the boat. There are a ton of potential opportunities out there. There are 27 tribes which make over $100 million a year...We need to get moving on them."

That hunger for money—both for personal and political ends— explains much about the casino-lobbying heist: The Indian casinos were really giant piggybanks for the two men to enrich themselves. Using a scheme that they dubbed "Gimme Five," the two men had persuaded six tribes to pay a total of $66 million from 2001 through 2003. The huge fees, which for some tribes rivaled what Fortune 500 companies spend yearly on their lobbying efforts in Washington, were paid to two of Scanlon's firms. The heart of the "Gimme Five" scam was surprisingly simple: unbeknownst to the tribes, Abramoff had cut a kickback deal with Scanlon to split most of the revenues between them, yielding them each almost $21 million in profits. They worked similar deals with different tribes, altering their methods only slightly.

Indian gaming started to take off after 1988, the year that Congress passed the Indian Gaming Regulatory Act, which opened the doors wide for new Indian casinos. For Abramoff, the casinos represented a jackpot that he exploited in stages. In the mid-1990s, early on in Abramoff's lobbying career, he won some big victories for his first client, the Mississippi Choctaws, but several years later he ripped them off when he had them hire Scanlon for extra help.

During the 2005 Senate hearings, Arizona Senator John McCain attacked Scanlon and Abramoff's treatment of their clients. The loss of money was bad enough, but at least equally if not more galling to the tribes' self-esteem were dozens of e-mails between the two men—and some of their colleagues—in which they referred to their tribal clients with contempt, calling them "troglodytes," "morons," "monkeys," and "imbeciles."

In looking back over Abramoff's career, he had a larger-than-life presence in Washington. He had long commanded consulting fees between $500 and $750 from an Israeli telecom firm and lavished gifts to so many senators and representatives that he became known by the moniker "Casino Jack." Although famed for his public fund-raising and wining and dining of members of Congress, Abramoff also was a stealthy operator who funneled millions of dollars through conduits and front groups to enrich himself and his political allies and chosen causes. He was a serial name-dropper. Yet he was regarded by many as a generous and philanthropic soul.

To win political friends, he used high-profile venues to cozy up to the powerful; he rented four luxury sports suites at Washington's leading football, basketball, and baseball stadiums that he rented for roughly $250,000 a year, the fees that were largely underwritten by Indian casinos and foreign clients. For extra clout, Abramoff became a restaurateur: in February 2002 he opened Signatures, an upscale eatery near Capitol

Hill and The White House that quickly became a popular hangout for members of Congress, staffers, and Bush administration friends, as well as a choice spot for holding GOP fund-raisers.

The Indian casino-lobbying game that Abramoff dominated for several years made him attractive to members of Congress who were on a constant hunt for campaign cash. At Abramoff's urging, several tribes expanded their giving to his GOP friends in Congress. At the zenith of his Indian casino-lobbying career, six tribes with casinos that Abramoff represented donated some $3.5 million in a three-year period, of which some two-thirds went to GOP members and campaign committees.

Clearly, Abramoff and Scanlon possessed a rare talent for exploiting others' weaknesses. They were on a constant search to take advantage of Indian wealth, and they could sniff out weak links. Scanlon sold the tribes on a project to develop a database to mount 'Operation Open Doors.' The database would provide enormous amounts of information to help the Indians work out their budgets. They paid $1.5 million for it only to find out later that its true value was less than $100,000.

In the end the whole scheme unraveled. The principal scamsters got varying prison terms, and the deception cast a dark cloud over many Republican legislators. Abramoff knew how to exploit both the naïve and those who should have known better. That was the kind of player he was, manic and diligent in all his pursuits.

Michael Milken and Junk Bonds

Michael Milken's star-crossed career began in 1970 when he joined the little-known Drexel investment firm on Wall Street and began to research and trade a new financial instrument dubbed, not without reason, junk bonds. He believed that the long-term reward in owning such high-yielding, low-quality securities far outweighed the risks. He built an empire by buying junk securities for himself and for investor clients, helping them in underwriting the issuance of the bonds for entrepreneurs and corporate raiders who were unable to easily raise capital from conventional sources such as banks.

In the mid-1980s, Milken provided vast amounts of monies for a generation of entrepreneurs. These professionals had a vision of major US companies as bloated and vulnerable to attack and takeover. That fueled widespread enmity against Milken in corporate America—and allegations that he was corrupting financial markets. He himself made

$500 million from his junk-bond empire in 1987. However, in 1989, Rudy Giuliani, then the US attorney in Manhattan, persuaded a grand jury to indict Milken on eighty-nine charges, including racketeering, insider trading, and securities fraud.

In April 1990 Milken with his business in a shambles after his indictment, pleaded guilty to six lesser charges that mostly involved violations of securities-disclosure rules.

He was sentenced to ten years in prison but served twenty-two months.

After his release Milken was diagnosed with prostate cancer. He received the grim news after insisting that his doctor test him for the disease because a friend had recently died from it. Diet and exercise became a new priority for Milken, who recovered from the disease and started a foundation that has raised more than $350 million for cancer research. He donated millions more for scholarship and education programs and launched the Santa Monica, California-based Milken Institute, an economic think tank.

There was such grim financial news that followed him when he left the business of investment banking. The landscape was littered with the ruins of a number of financial institutions, such as Columbia Savings and Loan of Beverly Hills and about fifty other banks. What caused their bankruptcy? They had large holdings of Drexel/Milken-issued high-interest, low-rated junk bonds. When a junk bond was adjusted on the books of the savings and loans to reflect their real market value because of a federal law, the institutions all sank into collapse. The real market value of their overall assets was so far below what they had paid that the value of their overall assets in relation to liabilities turned out to be below federally required levels.

Cities and counties and special revenue districts across the country bought investment contracts made up of Drexel/Milken bonds "guaranteed" by affiliates of both the First Executive Insurance Company and Milken. The losses on these instruments—losses directly borne by taxpayers in many cases—were in the billions. First Executive Insurance and so many other companies and financial institutions went out of business. Then the junk bonds started to default at the rate of 5 percent to 10 percent per annum, or about five to ten times the rate predicted by Milken and his friends and in business schools across America.

During his tenure at Drexel, Milken could and did raise vastly large sums for investors. He helped players like Boone Pickens and Carl

Icahn mount takeover raids on mammoth corporations such as Phillips Petroleum. He funded Ron Perelman in his takeover of Revlon. His ability to raise money so that relatively small players could attempt to seize power from far larger players was hailed by many in the halls of academe as a boon to American business. In fact, Milken was hailed as the man who ushered in a new era in the market for corporate control. Junk bonds were seen as the wave of the future!

All in all, the emergence of the Drexel-funded takeover boom together with a deficit-fed consumer spending spree along with a major fall in interest rates generated huge fees on Wall Street. The major investment banks and securities firms expanded at a stupendous rate. Starting salaries leaped into the mid-six-figure range for aggressive, hustling young investment bankers. The media praised Milken as a true financial visionary and guru. He had created a new financial instrument that was superior to existing instruments that made for a fine investment and in the process helped American industry grow, enabled management to be more effective, and generally made Americans in general economically better off.

These bonds were designed to pay a yield so high that even after deducting for the defaults that would inevitably occur, bond buyers would still be far ahead of where they would have been if they had bought boring old Treasury bonds with their nil default rate but much lower yields. The borrowers were said to have an advantage because with the proceeds of the Drexel junk debt, they could apply their ingenuity, talent, and their own innovations to make their businesses grow and grow. The American consumer was better off, so the common wisdom went, because the newer bonds would provide innovative kinds of goods and services.

So for all of Milken's revolutionary strategies for raising capital, why did Drexel Burnham face ruin and cause the default rates of close to fall to 10 percent a year in Drexel junk as well as face bankruptcy of large players and the criminal convictions of a number of substantial Drexel operatives?

As anyone who has ever applied for a loan knows, borrowers have to pay more interest if they are in shaky financial condition. In fact, borrowers not only have to pay more interest for "hard money," they are also willing to pay the "fixer" of the loan a far larger commission. Milken wanted that business and wanted it badly. Borrowers of, say, pension funds would have to show the advantages of their funds over treasury bills. When things were going well, they were happy to pay Milken his commission, feeling that this was money well spent. However, the flaw in it all was that Drexel bonds were not even close to as good a buy as Milken said they were. He claimed that defaults had absorbed only about 15 percent of the yield advantage, which had been available in the high-yield market. The other 85 percent had been gravy. The truth was that his bonds defaulted far more often than investment-grade bonds. It came out that his real rates of default were easily high enough to demolish the attraction of the bonds. And that rate would have been even higher were it not for his inventive measures of concealment.

Investors thought that they had conventional liquidity, but they learned that their bonds could be sold only at a price that many buyers were not inclined to pay. They were eventually faced with the problems of high default rates and illiquidity. But unfortunately what Milken did was continue to sell more bonds and use the proceeds to pay off the first bond issue. And then he used the proceeds of a third offering to pay off the coupons on the second offering, and the process just kept on rolling: a classic Ponzi scheme.

Milken also overfunded many of these loans, which meant that he raised more money for an issuer than they could use or even wanted. If the bonds in the first overfunded issuer's portfolio defaulted, that would likely mean a default by the original issuer. And a default of bonds means—or could mean—the end of a company. This is similar to what is likely to happen if one big issuer simply issues more and more debt to pay off his earlier debt and then the house of cards eventually collapses. As with all Ponzi schemes, it couldn't go on forever. But while it lasted, it was a miraculously simple way for Milken to pull buyers more or less out of thin air and thus create a market for his junk.

The issuance of junk bonds was the first and prime engine of business at Drexel/Milken. Over the ten years, from 1978 to about 1988, Drexel issued about $200 billion worth of bonds. The firm was paid about 3 percent as a minimum fee for this kind of work. It also got paid in warrants and equity kickers, which raised the rate to as much as 30 percent of the total equity capitalization of the bond-issuing corporation. The conventional broker earned a standard commission, which usually came out to a fraction of a percent of the total sale. This same broker also had to trade at current market prices dictated by the laws of supply and demand, which meant they might show a profit or a loss on the trade. But Milken could not only trade tens of billions at will, he could also fix both ends of the trade to give himself any level of commission or profit he wished.

The entire Milken money machine was fueled by an outright lie about the correct rate of default of the Milken-issued bonds. If the rate of default on his bonds was truly 1 percent per year as he claimed, Milken would have produced results close to magical proportions. However, if it were 3 percent or 4 percent or more, the Milken machine would soon run out of fuel and eventually blow up in a huge cloud of smoke. In fact, if the bonds had been adjusted for the correct level of default, except in very circumscribed circumstances, they would not be a better investment than treasury bonds.

Milken's bonds were not entirely worthless. If they had been kept in portfolios and a proper account taken of their likely real rates of default by means of reserves or charges against earnings, they would have been a legitimate investment—although nowhere nearly as good an investment as Milken claimed. But taken at Drexel/Milken's claimed value, using the phony default rates claimed by Milken, without accounting or reserving for losses, they were a catastrophe.

The claims that Milken junk bonds in some way added measurably to the well-being of the American economy was proven to be an outrageous falsehood. The dealings ruined lives: workers lost their jobs, pensions were emptied, and stockholders and bondholders from the hundreds of Drexel companies found the value of their investments vanish into thin air. In short, Milken rode roughshod over every ethical principle and every legal institution that was supposed to protect Americans and their savings.

Finally, Milken pleaded guilty to a number of what we generally call "white-collar" crimes. But in many ways his methods resembled those of organized crime. Before Milken, Drexel was a small but well-regarded firm doing its job much as other investment banks did theirs. When Milken took it over, it was transformed into an organization that was puffed up beyond normal scale by its sales of essentially fraudulent securities: the overpriced, incorrectly valued junk bond. Milken was bound to grow extremely rich by the sale and use of that item for takeovers, restructurings, insider trades, and greenmail. But it was eventually bound to fail as real rates of default caught up with inadequate reserves for loss.

The true similarity between Milken's methods and those of organized crime can be found in the mindset of Milken and how he and his colleagues applied the underworld tactics of the con and the shakedown, the swindle and the heist in the world of finance on both a national and international scale.

What is the Price of Success?

What motivated Milken and Abramoff? What got them going? How do we tease out the similarities and differences between them? In many ways they are different animals, and yet in many ways they are similar beings. Both received jail sentences, yet Abramoff was clearly the more criminal of the two. In effect, he flat out stole from the Indian tribes, and he knew what he was doing. It wasn't as if he was shocked by the investigation that led to his conviction. Milken, on the other hand, seemed not to have believed that he broke the law. Yet he certainly caused severe damage to many institutions, pension funds, and companies. The impact of overpriced junk bonds was astronomical in the bankruptcies that followed. Let's look more closely at the similarities between these two exploiters in order to get a fuller understanding of their methods.

From their college days, both sought out influential people with whom to align themselves. Milken became friendly with professors who later were instrumental in his progress in promoting junk bonds. Abramoff quickly rose through the ranks of the Young Republicans and made alliances with powerful people who later helped him in his lobbying efforts. Both men were fueled by an intense ambition, a relentless pursuit of money, and a need for aggrandizement.

Both Milken and Abramoff had supportive and close alliances with all kinds of important people. Abramoff could not rival Milken's ability to impact the financial world—this was not his turf. Yet he bilked the Indian tribes out of tens of millions of dollars. Both were convicted of breaking the law. Milken was indicted on ninety-eight counts of racketeering and securities fraud as the result of insider trading. But after a plea bargain, he pled guilty to six securities violations but was never convicted of racketeering or insider trading. Milken was sentenced to ten years in prison and permanently barred from the securities industry by the Securities and Exchange Commission. His sentence was reduced for cooperating with testimony against his former colleagues, and with good behavior he was released after less than two years.

Abramoff pled guilty to three criminal felony counts related to the defrauding of American Indian tribes and corruption of public officials. A Washington DC federal court found him guilty of trading expensive gifts, meals, and sports trips in exchange for political favors, and he was sentenced to a four-year term in prison.

The real link between these two was a vaunting ambition and arrogance. Within weeks of Abramoff's plea bargain, he told *Vanity Fair* that despite his mistakes and errors of judgment—which he attributed largely to his style of operating at breakneck speed—"I was the best thing [the Indians] had going." Abramoff then went on to boast about his powerful GOP friends and numerous lobbying accomplishments and why it was important to know him. Both of these men represented greed gone wild that crossed lines of ethical behavior. Ultimately, the scandals shed light on the potentially toxic mix of money and influence. An associate of Milken, Dennis Levine, was a trader at Drexel Burnham Lambert. He would often work his insider deals using a private line in his office. Regarding trading inside information on Nabisco stock in 1985, he told *60 Minutes* that every time the phone rang it was "like a cash register going off.

"No sooner did the stock open than my phone lit up like a Christmas tree, and each of the people involved called to say, 'How'd we do?' It was this incredible feeling of invulnerability, of a rush, that in pushing a button, in making two phone calls, I made close to three million dollars. And that's what drove it. That was the insanity of it all. It wasn't that hard."

Levine went on to describe how he managed to hide $12.6 million in a secret Bahamian bank account. The more money he made, the bolder he got and the easier it all became. Looking back, Levine realized he had a sickness. It had been an addiction. He lived for the high of making the next bigger deal. Levine never thought he would ever be caught, yet in the end he was: accused of making $12.6 million from insider trading. Levine later pled guilty to charges of securities fraud, tax evasion, and perjury. The manic drive and the excitement he described while he was riding high and the rush he got from living on the edge unites him psychologically with Abramoff and Milken.

When Levine said that the excitement was addictive he tells us a lot about how someone is sucked into making more and more money and gaining prestige in the process. Exhilaration merges into and is a part of such heightened emotions as euphoria and even ecstasy. Actor Laurence Olivier talked about this in his book *On Acting* when he described the emotions he felt in the days and hours leading up to an opening night—a kind of excitement that was extraordinary. Like a bullfighter, everything is geared toward the moment of truth with the audience.

So what really connects both Abramoff and Milken in their pursuits is this rush of excitement that entered their bodies like a drug that created a similar high. The challenge before them was taken on with a high arousal. There may have been dangers and threats and all kinds of other problems, but having entered into the arena willingly provided a kind of security and sense of control. Their level of self-absorption was so high that the question of whether they could pull it off didn't really arise or enter the mix. They were never on the defensive but on the offensive. That's why the excitement produced such aggressive behavior—it thrust them forward and forced them to reach out and reach for more and more. It got them to constantly expand their horizons.

At the same time, the excitement-seeking behavior provided them with a protective frame that shielded them from the usual doubts normal people have. This driven behavior produced such high levels of confidence and imbued them with a sureness of purpose.

Many of us are held back from pursuing risky, unethical, or even illegal activity because we sense some danger before us. Be it in relationships or careers, there are always boundaries that force us into a safe, if not retreat-like, mode. Yet with Abramoff, Milken, and other exploiters, boundaries exist to be trampled upon. In our everyday lives, we all face challenges. This type of exploiter, however, possesses a greater confidence level, and thus these exploiters' protective frame is more robust and they are able to face up to greater dangers while experiencing greater excitement. Paradoxically, danger and safety seem to go hand and hand, each feeding off the other.

We can use a similar analysis in understanding mountain climbers. According to the legendary American climber Smoke Blanchard, "The real reason I [take part in high-altitude trekking] is because of the charge...Because I get turned on. So that the greater the risk, the greater the joy" (Apter, 2007).

Or listen to the French mountaineer Maurice Herzog, celebrated conqueror of Annapurna: "A fierce and savage wind tore at us. We were on top of Annapurna; 8,075 meters, 26,493 feet. Our hearts overflowed with unspeakable happiness." For him this peak experience was enhanced by the dangerous conditions.

Obviously, work cannot provide as much risk and excitement as sporting activities. Apter relates the thrill of running with the bulls in Pamplona. Of course you must run faster than the bulls or they will gore you. Many feel that to run close to the bulls is a joy. In his book, *Iberia*, James Michener reports a discussion with a veteran bull runner who has shown him a horn scar across his chest: "'Is it something mystical?' he asked the runner. Matt looked at me as if I were out of my mind. "Christ, you miss the whole flaming point. It's fun! It's joy!'" He goes on to tell Michener that when the rockets go off and the black shapes come tumbling at you, hell, you have already made your commitment and all it takes now is a sense of joy...to be a part of the stampede.

No, this is not exactly the same rush that Dennis Levine experienced with making a fortune with insider trading or that Jack Abramoff felt when he was fleecing Indian tribes. But the basic principles are the same.

Donald Trump once said in an interview, "Everything in life to me is a psychological game, a series of challenges you either meet or don't." A game, of course, has rules. Exploiters who feel compelled to win at all costs have no compunction about breaking the rules and are either oblivious to or refuse to acknowledge the destruction they cause.

Why do some people go to extremes and take enormous risks that most of us would avoid, especially when these risks put them on the wrong side of the law? Whatever the reason, this kind of exploiter is seemingly incapable of remaining within the boundaries of acceptable behavior. It's not the ends that arouse the exploiter—it's the means. There are cases of businessmen who risk everything they already have in new enterprises when what they already possess is more than they could spend in a lifetime of the highest living. Aristotle Onassis put is like this: "Money becomes unimportant. What matters is success. The sensible thing would be for me to stop, but I can't. I have to keep aiming higher and higher—just for the thrill" (Onassis, p.107).

Maccoby (1973) defined a particular kind of corporate executive who found success in Silicon Valley. He called them the *Gamesman*: a type that is best defined as a person who loves change and wants to influence the course of events. They take calculated risks and are fascinated by new ways of doing so. They see developing projects, human relations, and their own career in terms of options and possibilities, as if it were a game. They are cooperative but competitive, detached and playful but compulsively driven to succeed; a team player but a would-be superstar; fair and unprejudiced but contemptuous of weakness; tough and dominating but not destructive. Their main goal is to be known as a winner, and their deepest fear is to be labeled a loser.

A study of the semiconductor components industry by Maccoby found that it is run by cool and daring gamesmen. Here we find executives who are highly imaginative gamblers. A series of intense competition for high stakes pervades the whole industry and is experienced on all levels. Maccoby also found that if they don't have enough excitement at work, they tend to enjoy playing poker or tennis games in which they can humiliate others by capitalizing on their weaknesses. Since they are so concerned about winning, the gamesmen tend to evaluate coworkers almost exclusively in terms of what they can do for the team or for themselves.

Note that both Abramoff and Milken surrounded themselves with the most powerful people in their professions. Like many adolescents, they craved a more romantic, fast-paced, semi-fantasy life, and this need led them to lose touch with reality and to lie—unconsciously or consciously—in an obsessive manner.

The most successful gamesmen are able to distinguish between the game and reality. But at their worst, gamesmen are unrealistic, manipulative, and compulsive workaholics. Their hyped-up activity hides intense self-doubt.

The most compulsive players must be continually "turned on," energized by competitive pressures. Deprived of challenge at work, they become bored and depressed. It is as if life is meaningless outside the game. Many people find high-pressure competition enervating and counterproductive, but for the gamesman it is the elixir of life. The Milkens and the Abramoffs of the world must feel as if they are outwitting you, that they are smarter and more creative than you. They live in a world where power, fame, success, and wealth constitute the supreme meaning of life. They will continue to play until they are stopped by society—when a judge tells them that the roller-coaster ride they've been on has broken down and they are then forcibly removed from the game. Then everyone is forced to pick up the pieces. Unfortunately for many, the pieces don't add up to much. Destruction follows soon after in the form of bankruptcies and severe losses of money.

Chapter Eight

Narcissistic Personality Disorder
The Trials and Tribulations of
Richard Nixon

Narcissistic Personality Disorder is a psychological diagnosis. It begins in early adulthood and shows itself in a number of contexts. Some of the outstanding features of the disorder are:

1) a preoccupation with fantasies of unlimited success, power, or brilliance.
2) a belief that one is unique and requires excessive admiration.
3) a sense of entitlement, i.e., unreasonable expectations of favorable treatment or automatic compliance of one's demands.
4) a need to take advantage of others to achieve one's own ends (interpersonally exploitative).
5) a lack of empathy: unwillingness to recognize or identify with the feelings and needs of others.
6) envy of others and/or a belief that others are envious of them.
7) arrogant, haughty behaviors and attitudes.

Exploiters often suffer from some aspects of this disorder. Like their comparatively normal counterparts, the narcissists are often intelligent and display great drive in achieving their ends. Unlike more typical people, they do not have much regard for those they may hurt. Many who suffer from this disorder possess an uncanny intuition in tailoring their behavior toward others in such a way as to win the day. They are often extremely likable, and most of us would consider their friendship to be a privilege.

Narcissists are drawn toward power and success but without a real need to treat the people around them in a fair manner. In fact, it seems that they often will go to any lengths to achieve their goals.

Unfortunately, such a man was Richard M. Nixon, who found his way to the apex of power—the presidency of the United States. Nixon achieved this position not without struggle but certainly through guile and double-dealing—the same qualities that would, in the end, bring him down. To begin to understand this complex man, we need to go back to the first time he won over the American people.

In July 1952 Dwight D. Eisenhower chose California Congressman Richard Nixon as his running mate. That fall a newspaper ran a story that alleged that Nixon was making use of a slush fund provided by donors who wished to curry influence with him. A number of Eisenhower's advisors urged him to drop Nixon from the ticket.

To keep this from happening, Nixon decided to plead his case on national television. In what became known as "the Checker's speech" Nixon, adopting the attitude of a man who had been grievously ill-used, adapted a solemn, hurt attitude in defending his actions and claiming that the only personal gift he had accepted was a cocker spaniel named Checkers for his children. It proved an effective performance. With Eisenhower sweeping to victory in November, Nixon became vice president at the age of forty. After serving under Eisenhower for two terms, Nixon was then was picked to run for president, losing the race in a tightly contested election to John F. Kennedy.

Let's for a moment imagine two friends popping open a couple of bottles of beer and settling in to listen to Nixon's famous Checkers speech.

"Oh my lord," says the first guy. "You have got to be kidding; there is so much lachrymose sincerity reeking from this guy."

"Yes," the second guy chimes in. "It's almost laughable with the way he is trying to play the role of the victim, the guy who is behind the eight ball and fighting for his life. You know this performance resembles some of the stuff he has done before in his previous campaigns."

His friend agrees. "But who is he trying to kid? He appears to me as an out-and-out liar. I wouldn't be surprised if his whole career wasn't built on lies. In all of those elections you mentioned he attacked his opponent with such smear tactics and low-level strategies. How can we believe him now? What I am really afraid of is what he will do when he gets this power. Certainly this speech will appeal to so many people that Eisenhower will have to keep him on the ticket. I realize now why they refer to him as 'Tricky Dick.'"

The other guy nods. "You know he should really have gone into acting. I'm not sure he is that good, but he ain't bad. I'm worried that he actually believes the stuff he's spitting out at us, and that's the dangerous part of the whole thing."

And indeed, years later, much of what these guys expressed about their fears came to fruition. Nixon prolonged the war in Vietnam while lying about the bombing of Cambodia. And of course, there was Watergate. Nixon was a consummate politician. Who else could have lost the presidency to John F. Kennedy in 1960, come home to California and then lost the race for governor, only to make yet another comeback in 1972, running for the presidency again, but this time winning?

The Beginning

Born in Yorba Linda, California, in 1913, Nixon attended Whittier High School and then Whittier College, also in California, graduating in 1934. He then took a law degree at Duke University, where he was elected president of the Student Bar Association and was admitted to the California bar in 1937. Returning to the city of Whittier, Nixon practiced law, becoming a partner in a local law firm in 1939. In 1940 he married Thelma Catherine (Pat) Ryan. In 1941 Nixon became assistant city district attorney. His legal career was interrupted by World War II, where he served briefly in the type-rationing section of the Office of Price Administration in Washington, DC, before enlisting in the navy. His four-year stint included a fourteen-month tour of duty in the Pacific. By the time he was discharged in 1946, he had reached the rank of lieutenant-commander.

Back home Nixon was approached by local Republicans who wanted him to challenge an entrenched liberal Democrat, Jerry Voorhis. He grabbed the opportunity and adopted a strategy that was to stay with him the rest of his life, which was to bad-mouth his opponent. He campaigned vigorously—characterizing Voorhis as voting the "Moscow" line in Congress—and took on his opponent in several debates. Nixon won by more than fifteen thousand votes. The people were won over by his charm. He was a forceful and energetic speech-giver. Once in the House of Representatives, Nixon established a reputation as an aggressive conservative with a marked anti-Communist bent. Appointed to the Committee on Education and Labor, he helped draft the Taft-Hartley Bill that outlawed the closed shop that mandated that unions had a right to organize within a company. As a member of the Committee on Un-American Activities, he achieved national fame for his interrogation of witnesses, especially of a State Department official, Alger Hiss, who was later indicted and jailed for perjury. That proved to be the launching pad for his successful run for the Senate in 1950 against Helen Gahagan Douglas. It was a hard-fought contest with both candidates trading insults. In the campaign he suggested that Douglas had Communist proclivities; he dubbed her "The Pink Lady," and again his campaign proved successful and he won by a wide margin. Then his fellow California senator resigned before the end of his term, allowing Nixon to gain seniority by replacing him.

When Nixon became vice president he was forty years old. He served under Eisenhower for two terms and then was picked to run for president. However, he lost the race in by a small margin to John F. Kennedy.

Afterward, Nixon retired to California to practice law and to write his memoirs. Two years after his unsuccessful bid for the presidency, he reentered the political fray, running for governor of California. When he lost, he told reporters, "You won't have Richard Nixon to kick around anymore, because, gentlemen, this is my last press conference." He practiced law again, this time in New York, and his law practice—along with royalties from the sale of his book *Six Crises* (1961)—provided him with an income he had not enjoyed before. He traveled to the Middle East, South America, and Europe—in France he was entertained by President Charles de Gaulle—and then he began to plan a resumption of his political career. He couldn't stay out of politics—his ambitions and character would not permit that.

Nixon campaigned for Republican Barry Goldwater in 1964, and in 1968 he sought the Republican nomination for president. He edged out his Republican opponents and won the nomination at the Republican convention in Miami. An early lead over his Democratic opponent, Hubert Humphrey, narrowed as the campaign progressed, but Nixon emerged the victor, albeit by a narrow margin of the popular vote. He was inaugurated as the thirty-seventh president in January 1969.

During the summer of 1972, the Democratic headquarters in the Watergate complex in Washington, DC, was burglarized. Though rumors of White House involvement circulated during Nixon's reelection campaign, they made little impact. However, early in 1973, the story of his involvement with Watergate began to achieve prominence. The men arrested for the break-in were convicted, and in order to avoid a maximum sentence, one of them offered to break his silence, claiming that certain White House officials had prior knowledge of the break-in. A Senate committee, under Senator Sam Ervin, began taking evidence. White House Counsel John Dean, implicated in the allegations, started giving evidence to Senate investigators. As testimony moved the plot closer to the Oval Office, the president requested and accepted the resignations of his two closest aides, H. R. Haldeman and John Ehrlichman, and dismissed Dean. In a televised testimony to the committee, Dean implicated Nixon in the cover-up. In July a White House aide revealed that Nixon had a voice-activated recording system in the Oval Office. Various attempts were then made to subpoena the tapes of the presidential conversations. Nixon initially resisted. In October Nixon ordered the firing of special prosecutor Archibald Cox Jr. Rather than carry out that order, Attorney General Elliot Richardson and Deputy Attorney General William Ruckelshaus resigned.

"The Saturday Night Massacre," as it came to be called, further undermined Nixon's credibility. Early in 1974 the House Judiciary Committee began to consider articles of impeachment against the president. In April Nixon released edited transcripts—1,254 pages—of his conversations. On July 24, the Supreme Court ruled that the president must hand over other tapes sought by the special prosecutor. Between July 27 and 30, the House Judiciary Committee approved four articles of impeachment. On August 5, the White House released transcripts sought by prosecutors, one of which—the "smoking gun" transcript—revealed that the president authorized a cover-up shortly after the break-in. Republican leaders in Congress told Nixon that he did not have enough votes to avoid impeachment. In a televised address on August 8, Nixon announced his resignation, and the following day, after a tearful farewell to staff at the White House, he departed with his family.

Themes of Nixon's Life

There are four critical moments in Nixon's career that most clearly highlight his style, if not his pathology: his run against Voorhis, his successful race for the Senate against Douglas, the Checkers speech, and finally, Watergate.

The Run against Voorhis

Running against Voorhis, Nixon worked out a campaign based on the premise that a vote for Voorhis was a vote for the political action committee of the Congress of Industrial Organization, which Nixon alleged was associated with Communist principles. Voorhis's supposed involvement in and endorsement by the CIO's political action committee, which was believed to be a Communist front organization, became a major issue in the campaign.

During a debate Nixon was challenged to produce proof of the allegation. He took from his pocket a local bulletin of the National Citizens PAC that contained an endorsement of Voorhis. Nixon was able to successfully link Voorhis with the PAC even though Voorhis had refused to accept the endorsement of any PAC unless it renounced all Communist influence. However, Nixon ignored that point in attacking Voorhis and defeated him by more than fifteen thousand votes.

Nixon's win over Voorhis was the beginning of a number of red-baiting campaigns by the future president. Voorhis later deemed himself the first victim of the Nixon formula for success. In 1958 Voorhis alleged that voters had received anonymous phone calls alleging that he was a Communist as well as newspapers stating that he was a fellow traveler.

In spite of any hard feelings, Voorhis sent Nixon a letter of congratulations in December 1946 and even met with the man who had defeated him. Voorhis was seen as a gentleman throughout his political career, while Nixon was beginning to get a reputation for being a street fighter who would use to any method to diminish the other guy in the eyes of the electorate. And of course, in those Cold War days, Nixon found the best way to accomplish this was by raising the specter of Communist affiliation.

Tricky Dick vs. The Pink Lady

Helen Gahagan *Douglas* entered politics in 1944. She was elected to the House of Representatives from California's fourteenth congressional district as a liberal Democrat and served three full terms. In 1950 she ran for the US Senate against Nixon, who used his tried-and-true Red-baiting strategy, hinting that she was a fellow traveler, citing as evidence her supposed Communist-leaning votes in Congress. He referred to her as "The Pink Lady," and his manager said that she was "pink" right down to her underwear. Nixon, together with his campaign manager, Murray Chotiner, printed fliers on sheets of pink paper to underline the point.

Not to be outdone by Nixon, Douglas coined a term for Nixon that would become one of the most enduring nicknames in American politics: "Tricky Dick." When Nixon won the election, with over 59 percent of the vote, Douglas's political career came to an end.

The Checkers Speech

As noted previously, in 1950, Nixon was elected to the US Senate and became an outspoken critic of President Truman's conduct of the Korean War; he also talked about wasteful spending by the Democrats and alleged that Communists had infiltrated the government.

But Nixon's rapid rise in American politics came to a grinding halt after a sensational headline appeared in the *New York Post* stating, "Secret Rich Men's Trust Fund Keeps Nixon in Style Far Beyond His Salary." The headline appeared just a few days after Eisenhower had chosen him as his running mate. Amid the shock and outrage that followed, many Republicans urged Eisenhower to remove Nixon from the ticket before it was too late.

Nixon, in a brilliant political maneuver, took his case directly to the American people via the fairly new medium of television. In a nationwide hookup, with his wife sitting stoically nearby, Nixon offered an apologetic explanation of his finances, including the now-famous line regarding his wife's "respectable Republican cloth coat" and the tale of the little dog named Checkers that had been given as a present to his young daughters. "...I want to say right now that regardless of what they say, we're going to keep it."

Nixon talked about how he and his family lived rather modestly, about how he paid eighty dollars a month and the family was saving up to buy a house. With Pat looking on, Nixon detailed their mortgaged home in Washington and the similarly mortgaged home in California, then occupied by his parents. He went on to say that every dime he had earned had been honestly won.

"Pat doesn't have a mink coat. But she does have a respectable Republican cloth coat," Nixon said.

Nixon expressed pleasure that the Democratic candidate Adlai Stevenson, whom he said had inherited wealth from his father, could run for president, adding, however, that people "of modest means" must also get a chance.

"Remember Abraham Lincoln, you remember what he said: 'God must have loved the common people—He made so many of them.'"

It is hard not to be impressed by the way Nixon was always at his best with his back against the wall. Confronted with exposure of an illegal campaign fund, his tactic was instinctive. He faced the nation on TV, struck a clean, all-American pose, and with chin forward grappled with the charges directly. He was brilliant, disarming, winning. The subtext of his speech was: You all could be as guilty as I. They are after me and after you. I am as small and helpless against them as are all of you. Here we can see how he plays in to theme of paranoia, a particular style in American politics.

Nixon's presentation was so sincere that he effectively identified himself with most working-stiff Americans who themselves felt victimized by the system and the privileged.

He began the speech by saying, "My fellow Americans, I come before you tonight as a candidate for the vice presidency and as a man whose honesty and integrity has been questioned."

Regarding the slush fund Nixon said, "It isn't a question whether it was legal or illegal, that isn't enough. The question is whether it was morally wrong. I say that it was morally wrong—if any of the $18,000 went to Senator Nixon." He used the third person, the same distancing device he would employ later as president.

"And now to answer those questions," he continued, "let me say this: not one cent of the $18,000...went to my personal use. Every penny of it was used to pay for political expenses that I did not think should be charged to the taxpayers of the United States."

He went on to say, "I know that this is not the last of the smears. In spite of my explanation tonight other smears will be made. Others have been made in the past. And the purpose of the smears, I know, is this: To silence me, to make me let up. Well they just don't know who they are dealing with...I intend to continue to fight. Why do I feel so deeply?..I think my country is in danger....I say, look at the record. Seven years of the Truman-Acheson Administration and what's happened? Six hundred million people lost to the Communists."

And it is at that point in the speech where he hit upon the winning formula: hammer away at the hysteria of the hour, which was the success of the Chinese Communists winning control in China. The response was immediate. Millions of telegrams poured in overwhelmingly demanding that Nixon stay on the ticket. When Eisenhower saw the speech, his immediate remark was "I would rather go down in defeat fighting with a brave man than to win with a bunch of cowards."

When Nixon confronted Kennedy in their first debate for the presidency in 1960, he accused him of being soft on Communism. Nixon pressed him: "If only you would admit that you were wrong, I would be the first to drop this issue." However, Kennedy was unruffled, and he rebutted this attack by offering Nixon a more accurate version of what he had said, along with the reasons and the logic for the varying positions he had taken.

Later Nixon wrote: "I recognized the basic mistake I had made. I had concentrated too much on substance and not enough on appearance. I should have remembered that a picture is worth a thousand words." So his version was that he had been too straight, too rational, too honest. Obviously, talking from the gut would have served him better.

The Frost-Nixon Interviews

Nixon resigned the office of the presidency without really admitting any guilt over Watergate. Two years later, in 1976, the English interviewer David Frost came up with an idea to interview Nixon on national television. He knew Nixon was a skilled lawyer who had denied complicity in the Watergate scandal. For Nixon, the Frost interviews were a chance to persuade the American people that he had been done an epic injustice—and to make upward of $1 million for the privilege.

Although Nixon's active role in the cover-up had been well documented, the absence of judicial prosecution had left the country with a feeling of unfinished business. To hear Nixon admit to high crimes and misdemeanors could provide a national catharsis, a closing of the books on a depressing episode of American history.

On May 4, 1977, forty-five million Americans watched Frost elicit a sorrowful admission from Nixon regarding his part in the scandal. "I let down my friends...I let down the country. I let down our system of government, and the dreams of all those young people that ought to get into government but now think it is too corrupt...I let the American people down, and I have to carry that burden with me the rest of my life."

In preparing for the historic confrontation, James Reston, an assistant to Frost, combed the volumes of evidence of Watergate for the interviews. He said that over the many months reading through the archives he came up with new evidence of Nixon's collusion with his aide Charles

Colson in the cover-up, evidence that he was certain would surprise Nixon and perhaps jar him out of his studied defensive stance.

Frost, a natural performer, knew how to change his role from inquisitor to confessor, to back off and allow Nixon's contrition to pour out. When Nixon was taken by surprise—as he clearly was by the new material—the whole tone of the interviews changed. At the climactic moment, after Nixon's admission, he quickly reverted to blaming others for his transgressions. However, this reversion to his basic character was cut from the final broadcast. In the public's eyes, Nixon would remain a sad, less-than-tragic, ambiguous figure.

The Heart of Watergate

Charles Rangell begins his book *The Mind of Watergate* with an intriguing psychological premise that highlights the Richard Nixon era of politics. He calls it the era of a "compromise of integrity." The malady, he wrote, was widespread throughout the entire population and was interwoven with a kind of neurosis emphasizing how issues of integrity were increasingly a central problem for many politicians.

The range of involvement of this comprised integrity involved not just Nixon but the forty or so men under him. Watergate became a defining moment in American history; the press gave it the name "the sick society," which related to a breakdown of morality, of integrity, of the ability or interest to act with honesty, and of truth.

It is in this context that the issue of courage is highlighted: not only in the sense of physical heroism but the ability to retain one's honor against the pressures of a surrounding group. Each of the men under Nixon faced this challenge and failed. Rangell was not talking about conscious lying, which Nixon did, and his men did too, or about the behavior of the narcissist or the more-overt criminal. He was alluding to the chronic everyday erosion of ethics—how the president's men were willing to surrender their individual judgments to the will of the leader.

After Watergate the syndrome involving the lack of integrity went back into hiding where it usually resides. The data that was once relevant became repressed and then forgotten in our minds. At the hearings Senator Howard Baker asked a witness early on, "Sir, did you not feel at any time that what you were doing was wrong? What happened to your basic instincts?" This prompted a commentator later that evening to remark, "Perhaps this question came closest to the heart of Watergate."

The parade of witnesses before the Senate committee included the era's bright young men: not the scholars, not first in the class or editors of a law review, but shrewd, ambitious, clever, bright, socially poised men—high on the ladder and moving up fast. They were models of what many of us would have wanted to become.

"The Watergate Complex" is more than a group of apartment buildings in Washington. It is a complex in the minds of men. It refers to the difficulty living with accepted values and of maintaining honesty in a corrupt environment.

Syndromes resulting from compromises of integrity are commonly found throughout our culture. Cheating has been absorbed into the practical realities of life. One need only think of attitudes toward income tax preparation or martial fidelity where double standards are accepted norms. Compromises become acceptable, to the self and others, compatible with and—we must admit—often promoters of success.

Conflicts of interests exist within all of us. Watergate, seen as representing a compromise of integrity, is as old as mankind. Power and ambition, like politics, have become bad words. A third such word is "opportunism." Power, ambition, and opportunism could be called the three horsemen of corruption.

At the Watergate hearings, Senator Baker asked young Herbert L. Porter, who served on Nixon's staff, "Did you ever have any qualms about what you were doing?..I am probing into your state of mind, Mr. Porter."

The answer came back uncomfortably: "I was not the one to stand up in a meeting and say that this should be stopped...I mean...I kind of drifted along."

The questioning continued.

Baker: "At any time did you ever think of saying, 'I do not think this is quite right, this is not quite the way it ought to be.' Did you ever think of that?"

Porter: "Yes, I did."

Baker: "What did you do about it?"

Porter: "I did not do anything."

Baker: "Why didn't you?"

Porter: (After a long pause) "In all honesty, probably because of the fear of group pressure that would ensue, of not being a team player."

The need to belong—to be a member of the team—is another primary aspect of human motivation. Only one man, Hugh W. Sloan, Jr. did leave. The others stayed for many reasons, including loyalty, ambition, and fear.

In her 1981 book *Richard Nixon: The Shaping of His Character*, Fawn Brodie, after looking at Nixon's life, became furious. She found that Nixon lied in matters large and small throughout his life. She contends that "Nixon lied to gain love, to store up his grandiose fantasies, to bolster his ever-wavering sense of identity. He lied in attacks, hoping to win....And always he lied and this most aggressively, to deny that he lied....Finally, he enjoyed lying."

Brodie referenced Nixon lying about such trivial matters as his college major, his wife's first name, and his birth date. He told bigger, more damaging lies as well, as in his first campaign for Congress against incumbent Jerry Voorhis, about his secret slush fund in the 1952 presidential campaign, and of course, in the Watergate cover-up. Brodie argued that "almost every one of Nixon's victories and political achievements save the elections to the vice-presidency has been won as a result of lying, attack or the unexpected and fortuitous death of others."

The Checkers speech is a prime example. We may listen to the speech today and find the emotional tone unctuous and revolting. But at that time Nixon knew it would sell. He had, as Brodie puts it, "the skill of a man who can profit successfully on the fringes of political graft."

This leads to the perplexing question why Nixon constructed his own failure. At the time of the Watergate affair he was standing at the pinnacle of his success.

The answer can be found in the pattern of unconscious ambivalence and guilt about power delineated in Freud's 1916 essay, "Those Wrecked by Success." Nixon unconsciously needed to fail in order to appease his guilt. Nixon turned his triumph into dust, destroying the power of which he unconsciously felt unworthy.

Did Nixon suffer from an exaggerated but not a pathological narcissism that we all share in to some extent? Lacking empathy toward others, he often sought revenge. Cruel toward his enemies, unprincipled and ruthless toward his opponents, Nixon was often self-sabotaging; his narcissism contained a strong component of masochism. A loner throughout his life, he had no true friends, not even his wife Pat, who he mistreated and humiliated and never really trusted. Devoid of empathy, Nixon had no authentic interest in the welfare of others. People were mere extensions of himself, necessary to function but not regarded as worthy of respect as separate and distinct individuals. Because of Nixon's envy, his narcissistic rage and paranoid fears, his constricted ability to feel emotions, he frequently exhibited self-defeating behavior.

A bad sport and an awful loser, Nixon was unable to admit defeat or take responsibility for his irrational and self-destructive decisions.

As a politician in the age of mass media, Nixon understood that political power rests on the capacity of the politician to gather and manipulate information. Politics, then, becomes akin to theater. Nixon had training as an actor. Presidential power has evolved into an exercise in swaying public opinion and the attempt to mobilize the masses through the construction of simple, powerful images. For Nixon and his associates, Watergate became an issue of public relations. Politics becomes severely distorted within such a conception, truth becoming a matter of indifference to the men exercising power. Once truth loses meaning, the political process loses its moral legitimacy. Politics then degenerates into utter banality, leaving a public resigned to thinking that all politicians are liars or crooks and consequently that political process does not matter.

Certainly, a major instance of Nixon's self-destructive and masochistic tendencies can be seen by the fact that he taped his own illegitimate activities. Why didn't Nixon just turn the tape recording system off? He knew he was recording incendiary material. What was he thinking? Did he expect to be able to edit the tapes later for his own purposes? Did he feel that safe? Was he careless? Was his judgment that bad?

Perhaps the tapes were an act of unconscious self-sabotage. In the narcissistic character, the need for admiration is so strong that the achievement of any one goal does not end that need. Narcissistic rewards can be extracted even from events that also bring suffering.

As mentioned earlier, a number of traits are assumed here: grandiosity, a feeling of omnipotence, and exhibitionism are all parts of it. Ambition and a craving for power, in the pathological sense, both traits of high intensity, accompany the narcissistic syndrome. All of these characteristics become the enemies of integrity.

President Harry Truman expressed a scathing a point of view about Nixon in Merle Miller's book *Plain Speaking*:

All the time I've been in politics, there's only two people I hate, and he's one. He not only doesn't give a damn about the people; he doesn't know how to tell the truth. I don't think the son-of-a-bitch knows the difference between telling the truth and lying...Nixon is a shifty-eyed goddamn liar and people know it. I can't figure out how he came so close to getting elected President in 1960...He's one of the few in the history of this country to run for high office talking out of both sides of his mouth at the same time and lying out of both sides.

Rangell points out that opportunistic, self-seeking, rule-breaking behavior, from the mildest to the most severe, takes place every day. The central thrust of Nixon's character was that whenever life presented him with the necessity of choosing between self-advancement at the expense of the truth as opposed to considering the well-being of others, he chose self-advancement.

Rangell goes on to say that the syndrome of the compromise of integrity is a kind of neuroses. Nixon knew right from wrong but had a desperate pressure to advance no matter what. He covered his overweening ambition with a cloak of patriotism and the good that he wanted to do for the country.

A combination of inborn traits and early-life experiences caused Nixon to develop a drive to achieve that invariably turned malignant and left a trail of victims in his wake. There was a wide disparity between his ambition and an always-shaky feeling about its fulfillment. Thus, even when success occurred it was never sufficient. In a story of young Nixon by Donald Jackson that appeared in the November 6, 1970 issue of *Life,* a classmate remembered seeing Nixon cheat during a college debate. He had been citing facts and figures from a piece of paper that was actually blank. From there to cheating on an exam in law school at Duke to Watergate where his actions went off the deep end, Nixon became his own victim.

Nixon himself was aggressive but not courageous, no more at the end than during the course of his career. He did not have the courage to trust the people, never feeling that they would like him if they came to know him. Chief Justice of the Supreme Court Earl Warren disclosed that he detested Richard M. Nixon with a most unjudicial-like short fuse.

"'Tricky,'" said Warren, "is perhaps the most despicable president this country has ever had. He was a cheat, a liar, and a crook, and he brought my country, which I love, into disrepute. Even worse than abusing his office, he abused the American people."

This young navy lieutenant with the proclivity for a specific type of behavior arrived home from the war in 1945 and conceived the idea that he could unseat a competent and popular young congressman in his hometown, Jerry Voorhis. In Nixon's very first political speech, made spontaneously to the "Committee of 100" Republicans that were interviewing him, he revealed the characteristic which was to be his from then on: a palatable untruth wrapped in a banal cliché. His answer to a question about his political philosophy was spontaneous: "I believe the returning veterans—and I have talked to many of them in the fox-holes—will not be satisfied with a dole or a government handout."

The fact is that Nixon was never near a foxhole but held a comfort-able administrative position in the rear echelons. He had not talked to veterans there or elsewhere about their political philosophies. The words came out smoothly and automatically, without guilt. What he said was close enough to reality not to be challenged. Above all, it was emotion-ally tinged and timed to perfection. It took the committee of Republican businessmen ten minutes to choose Nixon as their candidate.

Congressman Voorhis, who had an outstanding record for inde-pendent honesty and who had therefore made many enemies with vested interests, was a sitting duck as his loyalty, his patriotism, his very manhood were mercilessly attacked—never head-on but with innuendoes and half truths, always with apologies and noble-sounding preludes.

"I have been advised not to talk about Communism," Nixon said, "but I am going to tell the people of California...." He went on to allude to the fact that Voorhis sat safely behind a desk in Washington while he, Nixon, defended his country in the stinking mud and jungles of the Solomons. And now the political action committee of the CIO, a left-wing Communist front, was actively backing him.

This was false but effective. That group had not supported Voorhis, but had actually opposed him. At a strategic moment in a debate at which proof of this repeated assertion was demanded, Nixon waved a document in the face of his opponent, which would never be checked or countered. Voorhis was flustered and thrown off his game. Every honest statement he gave in reply made things worse. Nixon pressed on, claim-ing Voorhis had admitted guilt.

Nixon used the same tactic four years later in his senatorial race against Helen Gahagan Douglas. He called her "The Pink Lady" who voted along the same lines as the left wing congressman Vito Marcantonio. He went on to say that she voted with him a total of 354 times. He said that he stopped counting them and that the votes were always against the security of the country. The charges were repetitive, the same dose of poison administered in many different forms, but could never really be checked for their accuracy.

So we can trace the Watergate Nixon scandal back to the Voorhis campaign. Nixon's dirty tricks worked for most of his life, but in the end they destroyed him and did considerable damage to the country he claimed to love. A growing disbelief toward politicians enveloped the American populace. If you can't trust the people who are representing you in Washington, then who can you really ever trust? A sad story indeed.

Chapter Nine

The Psychopath Next Door
Bernie Madoff

When the story first broke about Bernard Madoff's multi-billion-dollar scam in late 2008, the country was stunned by its scope and amazed at how long he had been able to get away with it. A respected, highly personable, and seemingly responsible person was behind a scheme so large that it achieved the dubious distinction of being the world's largest Ponzi scheme.

It was difficult to come to grips with the dimensions of such a massive con job—and even more so with the man who was behind it all. Who was this Madoff anyway? Did anyone really know him well? His wife? Children? Brother? This man, after all, was a big noise on Wall Street, belonged to the most prestigious country clubs, and contributed to important charities. He projected such a successful aura that people would beg him to manage their money. How did he pull it off—and for so many years? And, as a Jew, how could he swindle, and in some cases bankrupt, major Jewish charities like Hadassah or the Simon Wiesenthal Center? How could Madoff cheat close friends and family who trusted and revered him? And perhaps most puzzling of all, how could Madoff do this year after year without experiencing excruciating anxiety caused by the constant the fear of being caught?

The answer to these questions is both simple and complex: Madoff is the psychopath next door.

Let's for the moment imagine an exchange between two spectators in the courtroom as a sentence is being passed on Madoff—a sentence that would put him behind bars for the rest of his life. The first man was struck by Madoff's personality; he had a kind of aura, something sparked in him, a definite charisma. In fact, the man found him memorable. The person next to him, a lawyer, must have sensed the man's thoughts. "Quite colorful, isn't he? Very stimulating," the lawyer said. "But let me tell you something else about him, and I'm not trying to be dramatic or to shock you. *That is not a human being.* Or let's just say that he is not completely human. Some essential parts are missing."

Later when the man read more about Madoff and the psychology of scammers like him, he began to understand how the mental disorder, the psychopathic personality applied to Madoff. Unless they have problems with their aggressive behavior, psychopaths are not violent people. However, they have a malformed conscience. They have no feelings of guilt or remorse no matter what they do; no limiting sense of concern for the well-being of strangers, friends, or even family members. Imagine no struggles with shame, not a single one in their whole lives. In other words, they are free from internal restraints with an unhampered liberty to do just as they please, with no pangs of remorse. This is conveniently invisible to the world, and this is what makes them so dangerous and even treacherous.

We are human to the extent that we are able to communicate with other human beings and identify with them on a number of levels. If people lack the ability to empathize with their fellow man, they must be regarded as less than normal. Something important is missing in the psychopath. The Madoffs of the world are not complete men; if anything they function as machines that can mimic the human behaviors and emotions to a T.

They walk among us. You might even know one, but since they present such a convincing facade of normality they are very difficult to recognize. They can even form what appears to be close connections with others. They know how to charm you. They can impress you as honest and truthful, worthy of trust and of love. But in the end their psychopathology, possibly more so than other mental disorders, threatens the safety, the serenity, and the security of American life. From the ranks of the psychopaths come those who practice the most venal forms of deceit and in the end have the influence to wreck and destroy people's lives. Unfortunately, when they are caught, it is always too late.

The Rise of Bernard Madoff

In certain rarified circles, Bernard L. Madoff was known as an affable, charismatic man who moved comfortably among power brokers on Wall Street and in Washington, a winning financier who had all the toys: the penthouse apartment in Manhattan, the shares in two private jets, the yacht moored off the French Riviera.

Although hardly a household name, Madoff secured a long-standing role as an elder statesman on Wall Street, allowing him to land on important boards and commissions where his opinions helped shape securities regulations. Along the way he snared a coveted spot as the chairman of a major stock exchange, Nasdaq.

And his employees say he treated them like family.

There was, of course, another side to Madoff. Reclusive, at times standoffish, this Bernie rarely rubbed elbows in Manhattan's cocktail circuit or at Palm Beach balls. This Bernie was quiet, controlled, and closely attuned to his image, down to the minutest details.

Madoff was, for instance, an avid collector of vintage watches and took time each morning to match his wedding rings—he owned at least two—to the platinum or gold watchband he was wearing that day.

Per his directives, the decor in his firm's New York and London offices was stark. Black, white, and gray—"icily cold modern," as one frequent visitor to the New York operation described it.

Despite nurturing a familial atmosphere in his offices, he installed two cameras on the small trading floor of the firm's London operations so he could monitor the unit remotely from New York. This Bernie also ran a money management business on the side for decades and kept it hidden far from colleagues, competitors, and regulators.

While he managed billions of dollars for individuals and foundations, he shunned one-on-one meetings with most of his investors, wrapping himself in a Wizard-of-Oz-like aura, making him even more desirable to those seeking access.

So who was the real Bernie Madoff? And what could have driven him to choreograph the $50 billion Ponzi scheme to which he finally confessed?

An easy answer is that Madoff was a charlatan of epic proportions, a greedy manipulator so hungry to accumulate wealth that he did not care who he hurt in order to get what he wanted. But some analysts say that a more complex and layered observation of his actions involves linking the world of white-collar financiers to the world of serial criminals.

Those analysts wonder whether good ol' Bernie Madoff might have stolen simply for the fun of it, exploiting every relationship in his life for decades while studiously manipulating financial regulators.

"Some of the characteristics you see in psychopaths are lying, manipulation, the ability to deceive, feelings of grandiosity and callousness toward their victims," says Gregg O. McCrary, a former special agent with the FBI who spent years constructing criminal behavioral profiles.

McCrary cautions that he has never met Madoff, so he can't make a diagnosis, but says Madoff appears to share many of the destructive traits typically seen in a psychopath. That is why, he says, so many who came into contact with Madoff have been left reeling and in a state of such confusion about their motives.

"People like him become sort of like chameleons. They are very good at impression management," McCrary says. "They manage the picture you receive of them. They know what people want, and they give it to them."

As investigators plow through decades of documents, trying to decipher whether Madoff was engaged in anything other than an elaborate financial ruse, his friends remain dumbfounded—and feel deeply violated.

"He was a hero to us. The head of Nasdaq. We were proud of everything he had accomplished," says Diana Goldberg, who once shared the daily twenty-seven-minute train ride with young Madoff from their homes in Laurelton in Queens to classes at Far Rockaway High School. "Now, the hero has vanished."

Of course, this "hero" never really existed. Madoff himself confessed that he was the author of a long-standing and wide-ranging financial charade.

During the decades in which Madoff built his business, he cast himself as a crusader, protecting the interests of smaller investors, bent on changing the way securities trading was done on Wall Street. He also actively wooed regulators who monitored his business. In that sense, Madoff was like a burglar who knows the patrol routes of the police and can listen in on their radio scanners.

"He once mentioned to me that he spent one-third of his time in Washington in the early 1990s, late 1980s," says a person who has known Madoff for years but requested he not to be identified because he does not want to be drawn into continuing litigation. "He was very involved with regulators. I think they used him as a sounding board and he looked to them like a white knight."

This individual adds, "He was smart in understanding very early on that the more involved you were with regulators, the more you could shape regulation...If you're very close with regulators, they're not going be looking over your shoulders that much. Very smart."

Madoff spent his early years in Laurelton, a close-knit Jewish enclave in Queens where he and his friends ate ice cream at the local Five and Dime and attended activities at the community center.

"It was an idyllic place to grow up in," recalls Vera Gitten, who attended elementary school with Madoff. She remembers him as "very thin," a good student, and extremely outgoing. Gitten recalls a musical skit that Madoff and his best friend wrote, rehearsed, and performed for the class when they were in fifth or sixth grade.

"It was a...'Sheik of Araby' kind of thing where they wore costumes, which were their parents' bed sheets, that made them look like they were desert sheiks," she says. "They would have us rolling."

None of Madoff's former elementary school friends could recall what his parents, Ralph and Sylvia, did for a living. But according to Securities and Exchange Commission documents from the 1960s, his mother had a brokerage firm called Gibraltar Securities registered in her name with an address in Laurelton. In 1963 the SEC began investigating whether a number of firms, including Ms. Madoff's, had failed to file financial reports and, if so, if that was cause for revoking their registrations. Early the next year, Ms. Madoff withdrew her registration and the SEC dropped its proceedings against her.

While Mr. Madoff's friends remember little about his parents, they clearly recall his childhood sweetheart, and future wife, Ruth Alpern, a pretty, bubbly blonde who was voted "Josie College" by her Far Rockaway High School class.

After graduating from high school in 1956, Madoff spent a year at the University of Alabama, where he joined Sigma Alpha Mu, a Jewish fraternity. A year later, he transferred to Hofstra University where he graduated in 1960 with a degree in political science. He later became a Hofstra trustee, but the university never invested with him.

Madoff spent the next year at Brooklyn Law School, attending classes in the morning and running his side business—installing and fixing sprinkler systems—in the afternoon and evening, recalled Joseph Kavanau, who attended law school with Madoff. When Kavanau married his wife, Jane, who was Ruth Madoff's best friend from Queens, Bernie was the best man.

"Bernie was very industrious," Kavanau explains. "He was going to school and working at the same time."

Madoff was never interested in practicing law, Kavanau says. Instead, he left law school and, using $5,000 saved from being a lifeguard and from his sprinkler business, joined the ranks of Wall Street in the 1960s.

"For many years when we were first married, my wife and I would go to their house or we would all go out to dinner, maybe a couple of nights a month," said Kavanau, who says that the first home Madoff shared with his bride was a modest, one-bedroom apartment in Bayside, Queens.

Over the years, however, the couples drifted apart. From time to time, Kavanau would turn on the television and catch a glimpse of Mr. Madoff—then a successful financier—being interviewed and realized that he had made his mark on Wall Street.

"The last time I saw him, we had run into him and Ruth on Worth Avenue in Palm Beach," Kavanau recalls. "We were definitely aware of how well he was living."

When asked if he could understand what happened or what may have motivated or prompted Madoff to take such risks after building up a seemingly successful business, Kavanau responded, "There is no way to explain it. I can't make it add up. It doesn't make sense," he says, growing increasingly frustrated. "I cannot take the Bernie I knew and turn him into the Bernie we're hearing about 24/7. It doesn't compute."

When Madoff arrived on Wall Street in the 1960s, he was an outsider. His small firm, Bernard L. Madoff Investment Securities, got its start by matching buyers of inexpensive "penny stocks" with sellers in the growing over-the-counter market. This hardscrabble market was made up of stocks that were not listed on the tonier, New York Stock Exchange, or the American Stock Exchange.

In the over-the-counter market, it was common practice—and completely legal—for firms like Madoff's to try to attract big trades to their shop by offering to pay clients a penny or two for every share they traded. His firm would make money by pocketing the difference in the "spread," or the gap between the offering and selling price for the stocks.

During the mid-1970s, when changes in the rules allowed his firm and others like it to trade more expensive and more prestigious blue-chip stocks, Madoff began gaining market share from the Big Board.

"He was a man with a good idea who was also a terrific salesman," says Charles V. Doherty, the former president of the Midwest Stock Exchange. "He was ahead of everyone."

While completely legitimate, the practice of paying for trading orders was entirely distasteful to blue bloods on the established exchanges, not to mention the fact that it was a threat to their livelihoods. It was around this time that Madoff began to cultivate relationships with key regulators.

"He was the darling of the regulators, without question. He was doing everything the regulators wanted him to do," says Nicholas A. Giordano, the former president of the Philadelphia Stock Exchange. "They wanted him to be a fierce competitor to the New York Stock Exchange, and he was doing it." In fact, his daughter married someone from the SEC.

Current and former SEC regulators have come under fire, accused of failing to adequately supervise Madoff and of being too cozy with him. Arthur Levitt Jr., who served as SEC chairman from 1993 to early 2001, has acknowledged that he occasionally turned to Madoff for advice about the market. But Levitt strongly denies that Madoff had undue influence at the SEC or that the agency's enforcement staff deferred to him.

Levitt said that he was unaware that Madoff even ran an investment management business and that Madoff never had special access to him or other SEC officials. He also noted that he and Madoff opposed one another on several key industry issues.

"The notion that Madoff came to my office many times is a fiction," Levitt says. "And the notion that he did my bidding is so fantastic that it defies belief."

Madoff's firm was an early adopter of new trading technologies. During the early 1990s, he served three one-year stints as head of the Nasdaq, an electronic exchange that had competed vigorously and won market share from brick-and-mortar exchanges like the American Stock Exchange (now NYSE Amex Equities).

Despite this flair for innovation, Madoff routinely told his employees to adopt the mantra "KISS" or "Keep it simple, stupid." He was, after all, a man of precise, controlled, and expensive habits. He smoked Davidoff cigars, had his suits custom tailored at Kilgour on Savile Row, and bought many of his watches at Somlo Antiques, an upscale London purveyor of timepieces.

Associates and others acquainted with him said his punctilious ways sometimes veered into obsessive-compulsive behavior. His office, for example, always had to be immaculate. According to a former employee, who requested anonymity because of continuing litigation and because, he said, regulators have told Madoff employees not to speak to the media, Madoff compulsively scoured the office for dirt. Once, in the New York office, he spotted an employee eating a pear at his desk. In the process, some juice dripped onto the gray carpet, this person said.

"What do you think you are doing?" this person recalls Madoff demanding. "Eating a pear," the employee replied. Madoff then ripped the soiled carpet tile from the floor and rushed to a closet to retrieve a similar swatch to replace it.

Julia Fenwick, who was the office manager for Madoff's London operation from 2001 until the unit was shuttered in December 2008, said that "everything had to be perfect" and that "you never left paper on your desk—ever."

Although he visited the London office only a couple of times a year, usually on the way to his vacation home in France, Madoff still reveled in micromanaging everything, including the office decor.

He redecorated his London office, spending about $700,000 for a refurbishment that recreated the black and gray decor of Madoff's New York office and his private jet, Fenwick says. The result was office furniture made from black ash, black trimming on gray walls, black computers, black mouse pads, and even a black refrigerator on the trading floor. But former employees and friends say Madoff's obsession with order and control of his environment never led them to suspect him of any underhanded activity.

"He appeared to believe in family, loyalty, and honesty," said one former Madoff employee. "Never in your wildest imagination would you think he was a fraudster."

Despite all of the money that rolled into Madoff's firm for much of its existence, financial pressures began to emerge in 2000 after Wall Street changed the way securities were priced and as new competition emerged. In his asset management business, however, Madoff continued to haul in fresh rounds of money from unsuspecting investors hungry for the predictable and handsome returns he booked year after year.

Veteran employees in the New York and London offices deemed it a privilege to invest with Madoff, according to people who worked at the firm. Some employees were said to have given Madoff a large portion of their life savings—all of which now appears to be gone. Like so many others who invested with him, his employees weren't lured to his funds simply by a promise of outsize returns. Rather, they say, they sought the security of investing with a man they knew and trusted: the Bernie they thought they knew.

The Psychopathic Personality

"Typically, people with psychopathic personalities don't fear getting caught," explains Dr. Meloy, author of a 1988 textbook, *The Psychopathic Mind*. "They tend to be very narcissistic with a strong sense of entitlement." As a result, they have a feeling of invincibility that precludes fears of their misdeeds being uncovered.

Madoff's seeming lack of anxiety about the scam he was running reminds J. Reid Meloy, a forensic psychologist, of criminals he has studied, and some forensic psychologists go so far as to see similarities between Madoff and serial killers like Ted Bundy. They say that whereas Bundy murdered people, Madoff murdered people's financial lives and their trust in others. Like Bundy, Madoff used a sharp mind and an affable demeanor to create a persona that didn't exist and then was able to lull his victims into a false sense of security.

Television footage of Madoff entering his apartment building on East Sixty-Fourth Street after federal authorities charged him with fraud didn't show a man exhibiting any sorrow or regret. With a battery of reporters asking him whether he felt remorse, he declined to respond and pushed his way into his building. (At that time his only public apology had not been to the victims whose lives he ruined or to the charities he bankrupted, but to his fellow tenants who were inconvenienced by the media circus outside their building. The apology was made via copies of a letter left in the lobby.)

Like McCrary, Dr. Meloy cautions that he has not met Mr. Madoff and can't make a clinical diagnosis. Nevertheless, he says individuals with psychopathic personalities tend to strongly believe that they are special.

"They believe 'I'm above the law,' and so cannot be caught," Meloy says. "But the Achilles' heel of the psychopath is his sense of impunity. This is what eventually will bring him down."

Meloy says it makes complete sense that Madoff would have courted regulators, even if he ran the risk of exposing his own actions by doing so.

"In a scheme like this, it's very important to keep those who could threaten you very close to you," Meloy explains. "You want to engage them as allies and shape how they go about their business and their attitudes toward you."

The fact that Madoff fooled regulators for decades was surely a "heady, intoxicating" feeling that fueled his sense of entitlement and grandiosity, McCrary says—a state of mind reinforced by the fact that his victims were well-educated and sophisticated people from the Jewish community, charities, public institutions, and prominent investor networks worldwide.

That's why McCrary thinks it's not so farfetched to compare Madoff to serial killers. "With serial killers, they have control over the life or death of people," McCrary explains. "They're playing God. That's the grandiosity coming through. The sense of being superior. Madoff is getting the same thing. He's playing financial god, ruining these people and taking their money."

A report from an investor who was ruined by Madoff went like this: "The phone in our apartment rang and it was my wife Sarah who answered. What the person said on the other end was both simple and devastating. We were financially wiped out. She replied, 'You're joking? This is a joke, right?'"

The investor went on: "We didn't know it yet, but we had been playing in the Bernard Madoff Investment Securities LLC Fantasy Financial League. It began when we sold our home at the peak of the market, collected what was left from an old divorce, found other monies, and then, with a combination of pleasure and trepidation, handed over our life savings to someone named Stanley Chais, the Los Angeles network organizer for a man named Bernard Madoff.

"Of course, we never heard the name Madoff—which has a peculiarly Dickensian ring now—and had no idea how he achieved such fantastic returns over the past forty years. All we knew was that my wife's entire family had been in the fund for decades and lived well on the returns, which ranged from 15 percent to 22 percent. It was all very secretive and tough to get into, which, looking back, was a brilliant strategy to lure suckers. Unlike the usual Ponzi mechanics, the fund even stopped investments into accounts a few years back, at least in our network."

"There were the usual warnings prior to investing—we all knew it was a risk, we were told to make sure we were diversified, blah-blah—but, my God, it had been going strong for so long and with such fantastic returns, we had to get in. The Securities and Exchange Commission even gave Madoff a clean bill of health several years ago. Well, maybe not a clean bill, but it didn't shut him down either. In the topsy-turvy world of investment, we were quietly, richly safe until this happened.

"I think everyone knew the call would come one day. We all hoped, but we knew deep down it was too good to be true, right? I mean, why wasn't everyone in on this game if it was so strong and steady? We deluded ourselves into thinking we were all smarter than the others. When it came to the investment game, we had it figured. And what was the game anyway? The way it was vaguely described to us was that the 'New York people' had a system whereby they placed a series of instant trades—at once with futures, currencies, and stocks—and out of this magic recipe fell a tiny 1 percent guaranteed, no-risk profit for the group. You do that twenty times a year, take away management fees and, wow, a steady 15 percent return. Man, these guys were good.

"But of course the call did come, as it always does with such things. It was not an ordinary Ponzi scheme we were all part of; it was the biggest in the history of the world, valued at some $50 billion. Lucky us. Small investors, institutions, hedge funds, global banks, pension funds—all fell victim to usual suspects: a smooth huckster and greed.

"You never want to hear the words that come with such a phone call. 'We are all wiped out.' But they came, and we went numb. We lost, on paper, $1.2 million. My wife's family's combined losses are close to $30 million. We're talking old ladies and men, lawyers, children with Madoff trusts, students in college, and an array of others who thought they had the world beat—and they did, at least for a time.

"Now, we, they, everyone in this fraud, are all wiped out. It's the kind of news that's been known to cause shortness of breath, sudden cardiac arrest, revolvers pulled from bedside drawers. It harks back to December of 1929 and the image of bodies falling from buildings. But what can you do?

"There's a line from *The Shawshank Redemption* that is apropos. It's spoken by Tim Robbins's character:

'Get busy living or get busy dying.' We've lost it all, but we're choosing to get on with living."

Bernie's Inner World

It is important to look at the inner life of a psychopath such as Madoff. Until Madoff was caught he looked like such a wonderful guy with a knack for making money. He was seen as being on top of his game and offering great returns to those people wanting to better their lives. A few were suspicious, feeling that the consistent returns Madoff generated for his clients were too good to be true. But they were ignored. The investors not only believed in him but actually felt privileged to have the opportunity to entrust Madoff with their money. Remember, he didn't make it easy for investors to give him their money—which only intensified their desire to be among the elite who did. And then he made them feel as if he were doing them a favor.

Let's get back to the profile of the psychopath: there is a superficial charm and keen intelligence, an absence of delusions or other signs of irrational thinking, a lack of remorse or shame, possibly an incapacity to love, and an impersonal and poorly integrated sex life.

The psychopathic personality represents a severe form of a narcissistic personality disorder. They are chronic manipulators always on the lookout to put something over on the other person. Remember the narcissist has a grandiose sense of self-importance and a special sense of entitlement. The psychopath is an extreme case of this disorder. However, a diagnosis is never really an explanation—it does more to categorize someone. In each of the cases I presented, I tried to highlight particular aspects in their personality that gave them some uniqueness. Many were out-and-out crooks but with slightly different pieces of character. For example, both Dreier and Madoff share similar characteristics. They both committed fraud, lied, and cheated others. Yet they were different human beings. Dreier viewed the world as a jungle and certainly was more aggressive. What they did share was their lack of empathy and as well as the ability to recognize or identify with the vulnerabilities of others.

Madoff's superficiality, callousness, ruthlessness, lack of loyalty, and his exploitive behavior become understandable in terms of his narcissistic personality structure. He must be omnipotent. The feeling of power he derives from this fantasy is a way of propping up his all but nonexistent sense of self.

The main clinical feature of this kind of the psychopath—whether they are a businessman, administrator, or out-and-out con man—manifests itself as a compulsion to "screw" the other guy, which creates the rush the psychopath derives from that action.

Madoff felt a high level of exhilaration during the years when his deception was working. He had such contempt for the victims of his scheme, looking down on those he so easily influenced and living his grand life while bilking them out of their money. The key to his behavior may be simple: Madoff was so delighted with his scheme that he saw no reason to stop. His corrupt activities were acceptable so long as his public image remained clean.

But digging deeper, we find in Madoff a kind of perverse character. The perverse state of mind acknowledges reality but at the same time is able to deny it. It engages others as unwitting accomplices and turns a blind eye in the abuse that is being perpetrated. Abusive cycles are set up where corruption breeds more corruption because of the complicity of the accomplices who wanted to believe so much in Bernie's scam.

According to the *Random House Dictionary* (1988), the word *perverse* is defined as "willfully determined not to do what is expected... evil, bad sinful." Perversion is not just a deviation from normality, but it represents a serious flaw in one's character. Freud analyzed the myth of Narcissus in which a beautiful young man looks into a lake and is mesmerized by the "other" beautiful youth. Narcissus's tragedy was that he did not realize that it was his own reflection that excited him. Unable to leave the beauty of his reflection, Narcissus died.

Its implication is that all gratification only comes from within us. In the myth, the characteristic of individual pleasure at the expense of others might be seen as selfishness in everyday life, except that in the pathological state of perversion, the self is not always present in the usual sense that self and the other are distinct entities. The selfishness of the perverse position recognizes others not so much as other distinct selves but as objects to be used for their own pleasure.

In Stendhal's novel *Le Rouge et le Noir* (*The Red and the Black*, 1830), there is a classic narcissist in the character of Mathilde. Says Prince Korasoff to Julien Sorel, the protagonist, with respect to his beloved girl:

"She looks at herself instead of looking at you, and so doesn't know you. During the two or three little outbursts of passion she has allowed herself in your favor, she has, by a great effort of imagination, seen in you the hero of her dreams, and not yourself as you really are." (Page 401, 1953 Penguin Edition, trans. Margaret R.B. Shaw)

Madoff used people to buoy up his self-esteem, but he never saw them as distinct individuals, hence his absence of feelings of guilt.

Secondly, the perverse state of mind acknowledges reality, but when it threatens the person's self-interest, they are also able to suppress it. It enables them to institute parasitic relations with others. So one side of the personality sees things for what they are while the other is locked into a mode of delusional thinking. The deluded, denying side can always claim its hold when reality is too painful.

Freud developed this idea from his original analysis of fetishism. A fetish takes the place of another object. Freud originally exemplified the concept by theorizing that boys need to deny the fact that the mother does not have a penis because if the child were to accept beings without penises, the possibility could exist that he might be deprived of his. The sexual fetish rests on the child's ability to set reality aside and retain the fantasy of the mother with the penis (the phallic mother). Thus, the shoe fetishist, for instance, originates with the boy's averted gaze from the fearful sight of the mother's lack of a penis. He looks to her feet, restoring his belief that mother is endowed with a penis, and his fears are allayed.

As that child grows into adulthood, the primal conflict continues, manifesting itself in different forms but always with the psyche knowing and not knowing, shifting between the two positions when reality becomes unbearable.

Without this defense mechanism, how could Madoff have operated his Ponzi scheme for so many years? When the fear of being caught became too stressful to bear, the denial mechanism kicked in and the fantasy world in which he was living took hold. The perverse mind becomes both a defense against these feelings and a source of satisfaction that everything will be fine.

Certainty is propped up when there is an agreeable accomplice. "Bernie you are the best," his grateful clients would say. The accomplice may be woven into the perversion—a sadist needs a victim. Perverse relationships between members of an organization bind them to one another and often to a leader in ways that ensure loyalty, as in the case of Enron.

We certainly make use of others in non-perverse ways if we recognize their rights and interests. However, in perverse relationships, use and abuse become merged. The perverse state of mind can be shared by a society when it turns a blind eye to abuse, as in the case of the Guantanamo Bay prisoner abuse.

Relationships between people range from mutual recognition and respect to disregard and then abuse. A mature society rests on mutual recognition and respect. The perverse state of mind, by comparison, is aimed at nullifying ethical considerations. Therefore, perverted solutions triumph over the destruction of barriers, boundaries, and differences.

Madoff's crime was so devastating because of his complete lack of empathy and concern for his friends, family, and investors—many of whom fell into all three of those categories.

Now that he is incarcerated for the rest of his life, we may wonder about his state of mind. In an interview with Madoff that appeared in *New York* Magazine in March 2011, we get that chance, but we must look closely at what he chooses to tell the interviewer.

Madoff tells the interviewer that nothing justifies what he did and that he can't bear the thought that people think he's evil. He said he cried for two weeks when he found out that his son, Mark, committed suicide on the third anniversary of his father's arrest and that he felt terrible when the media blasted his family. Madoff goes on to say that he had more than enough money to support his lifestyle but once he started the Ponzi scheme he could not extricate himself from it, so in essence he became a criminal near the peak of his legitimate success. But when the market started going downhill he needed to continue to produce similar 15 percent to 20 percent returns.

In essence, Madoff's defense is that he became a criminal in order to help his clients keep reaping the same benefits. According to Madoff, he just couldn't let these clients down.

Madoff then went on to say that he worries about his family and he worries about his victims although he is confident that they will be OK. Most of his victims, he rationalizes, "will get a substantial amount of their money back...It will be fifty cents on the dollar, but they probably would've lost all that money in the market."

Madoff then employs the tried and true "everybody does it" defense. He says in an offhanded way that the whole government is a

Ponzi scheme. He says that other investment firms should have known what he was doing—that they all are a bunch of crooks.

Notably lacking in the interview are any expressions of remorse on Madoff's part for the individuals and charities he destroyed. It is all rationalized in his mind, enabling him to live with himself.

This is the true manifestation of the mind of the psychopath—a person so detached from his fellow humans that he is essentially not quite human himself.

Chapter Ten

Women Stalkers, Femme Fatales, and As-If Characters

In reviewing the many incidents of fraud, insider trading violations, and imposture and deceit that we have seen in previous chapters, it is obvious that women are underrepresented. They are rarely caught in any bribery scams, Ponzi schemes, or overt corporate violations. Obviously, gender differences must play a major role in this disparity. This is not to say that women are innately more honest or less deceitful than men, only that they work out these baser instincts in different ways. Yes, it is rare that you will find a woman who approaches the deceit of a Madoff, a Dreier, or even Abramoff or Milken. Remember, at Enron it was all about the men. In fact, it was a woman who wrote a memo exposing the mammoth fraud. Yes, traditionally, women have been exploited as opposed to being exploiters. But in the cases where women are the exploiters, one dynamic does stand out: female stalkers who have been shown to be personally abusive and capable of destructive behavior as well as femme fatales who lead men down a one-way alley.

Orit Kamir, in her 2000 book *Maintenance of Cultural Myths: The Case of Stalking*, shows striking contrasts between fears caused by female stalkers and those that are generated by male stalkers. When women do the stalking, society sees it as subverting patriarchal sexual norms. Female stalking creates a sense of danger and social instability— it defuses male power. This dynamic can often be seen in films. *Play Misty for Me* and *Fatal Attraction*, to name two, involve active, erotomanic female stalkers who act out a script consistent with the emergent feminist views of the time. The films undermine patriarchal illusions and assumptions of male chauvinism and supremacy and deconstruct the male-active/female-passive ideas of gender relationships.

Play Misty for Me

Play Misty for Me marked Clint Eastwood's directorial debut, and quite a movie it was. Released in 1971, the story concerns a late-night disc jockey, Dave Garver (played by Eastwood), who is stalked by a female fan, Evelyn Draper.

Dave is a handsome womanizer and late-night disc jockey living in Northern California. Usually, after work, he stops for an early-morning beer at a local bar for a nightcap, after which he jumps back in his Jaguar XK150 and drives home to get some sleep in his spacious home in the woods by the ocean.

Late one night at the bar, Dave meets Evelyn, an attractive, mini-skirted young woman. Dave buys her drink, and the two hit it off. At some point he recognizes Evelyn's voice as belonging to the woman who phones the radio station every night asking him to play the Errol Garner jazz song "Misty" for her. Dave takes Evelyn home but, before having sex, warns her that he is in love with another woman.

"I'm kind of hung up on one (girl)...And you don't want to complicate your life," he says.

Evelyn's response is typical of that of a 1970s liberated woman: "Neither do I. But that's no reason we shouldn't sleep together tonight if we feel like it."

But in the days after their encounter, Evelyn develops the disturbing habit of dropping into Dave's house unannounced. When he tries to discourage her, Evelyn transforms herself into an ugly shrew, shrieking, "And what am I supposed to do? Sit here all dressed up in my whore suit waiting for my lord and master to call?

"Nobody asked you to wait for anything!"

"You're not dumping me! You're nothing! You're not even good in bed! I just felt sorry for you, that's all! Bastard! You poor, pathetic bastard!"

Dave is terrified by this outburst and attempts to reason with her, but Evelyn is nothing if not persistent and, refusing to be discarded, begins to shadow his every move.

Besides interfering with Dave's social life, Evelyn intrudes on his professional life, crashing a business lunch with a broadcasting magnate, who happens to be a mature, attractive lady.

"Is that your idea of a dish? She is a little old for you, isn't she?" Evelyn shrieks. "What is this, 'Be Kind to Senior Citizens Week?'"

Evelyn becomes progressively more possessive and eventually dangerous. After several perverse assaults on Dave, Evelyn, assuming the name Annabel, manages to become a roommate to Tobie, who is Dave's girlfriend. Evelyn ultimately kidnaps Tobie and holds her hostage. She then calls Dave and tells him she is in the San Francisco airport, about to leave for Hawaii, and is sorry for what happened, and she quotes two lines of poetry: *"And this maiden she lived with no other thought—than to love and be loved by me..."*

After the call, when Dave is alone in his broadcasting studio, he figures out "Annabel's" identity after remembering the poem by Edgar Allan Poe, "Annabel Lee," and reading the verses preceding the quotation: *"It was many and many a year ago—in a kingdom by the sea—that a maiden there lived whom you may know—by the name of Annabel Lee..."* Dave becomes frantic. When he calls Tobie, Evelyn answers the phone and "invites" him to Tobie's house (where Tobie is already bound and gagged with her hair cut off). Dave jumps into his Jaguar and speeds toward Tobie's place, which also overlooks the ocean. The house is dark and silent, and Evelyn waits with a butcher knife in hand

In a chilling climactic scene of *Play Misty for Me,* Evelyn attacks Dave with a knife on the edge of the cliff, slashing him several times. He manages to defend himself, and as he punches her in the face, she reels back and falls over the cliff to her death. Ironically, a taped version of his radio show, with Evelyn's request to play "Misty" for her, can be heard in the background. Dave and Tobie, who is at his side, leave the house together, wounded and supporting one another.

Psychology of the Film

Play Misty for Me succeeds primarily as a psychological study of the different forms of mental illness that can follow the state of mind generally described as "being in love." It depicts the conflicts inherent in maintaining close personal relationships, the difficulties we all face with intimacy, and the inevitable envy and jealousy that must be borne when we fall in love. Evelyn is driven to focus her attention on exploiting the object of her desire, namely Dave. Evelyn forms a delusional idea that this man is in love with her despite all evidence of his lack of interest in her. She is capable of destroying herself and others in pursuing him. She is unable to relate to the demands of external reality and her possessive, obsessive, morbid jealousy and envy lead to extreme violence and murderous behavior.

In the course of Evelyn's monomaniacal pursuit, she is willing to contemplate eliminating all those who dare to threaten her delusional belief system. Evelyn is willing to do anything—including committing murder—to revenge the self-inflicted injury which results from the realization that the object of her obsession dares to have an independent mind and a life of his own. Evelyn truly believes that without Dave her life is empty, if not worthless.

In Evelyn's mind, the fact that Dave played her favorite song on the radio whenever she requested it created a special relationship between them and that her desires, however unrealistic or pathological, could be magically fulfilled.

Evelyn ignores the fact that Dave does not know her personally, that he has many listeners in his audience, and that he has friends and colleagues. External reality for Evelyn is progressively replaced by a world of fantasy in which no interference is permitted.

Dave is good at his job, which combines his love for jazz and poetry, and he is able to touch the lives of people as he relates to them through the airwaves. He helps them, as well as himself, to get through the loneliness of the night or to overcome the loneliness of the day. One can imagine him having many fans who listen to, appreciate, and are touched by his soothing and sonorous words and who feel that he is almost a part of their lives. His success leads him to being sought after in his field. Dave lives a carefree life with no strings attached. It is true that he is a womanizer who has difficulty in sustaining close, intimate relationships, but we also get to know of his capacity for self-reflection and regret and of his growing capacity for guilt about his unfaithfulness to the woman he loves. Dave is an attractive character, who is in many ways flawed but also indulged by his friends, who seem to like him despite his faults.

Random House Dictionary defines the verb *to stalk* as: "to pursue or approach game, an enemy, etc., stealthily or furtively." In the definition, two types of people are mentioned: the "game" and the "enemy," illustrating the double register of such an activity, insofar as stalkers experience their victims as the targets of an exciting sexual game of conquest and, at the same time, of a destructive hate-filled attack. Once the stalker gets the victim in her grasp, there is no way she is able to let go of her prey.

The major feature of Evelyn's pathology is her belief that her fantasy relationship with Dave is real and not one only played out through the airwaves or inside her mind. This belief cannot be thwarted, even when external reality refutes the idea. The internal fantasy drives Evelyn forward and compels her to act as she does, while she loses all awareness and insight that she is acting on delusion rather than reality.

Having tracked Dave's habits and movements, Evelyn orchestrates a first encounter with him in the safety and familiarity of his local bar, with its friendly bartender, Murphy, looking on. Flattered by Evelyn's attention, Dave is easily lured into chatting with her. He recognizes her voice from the radio, and she confesses to being a fan who listens to him all the time.

The day following their first encounter, several telling signs of Evelyn's disturbed personality emerge. She arrives unannounced at his doorstep, carrying bags of food to feed him. When Dave shows that he is annoyed by such an intrusion, she emotionally collapses and asks him to decide on her behalf whether she should go or stay. He misreads the situation and feels convinced he must reciprocate her passion and lets her cook for him. But when Dave's response does not match Evelyn's expectations, she starts feeling persecuted and overreacts to the situation. She panics at the idea of being abandoned and backs off, which enables Dave to relax and feel less threatened.

Evelyn repeatedly visits Dave's home, almost delusionally convinced that he is with another woman. Dave is repulsed by her behavior and morbid jealousy and tries to dissuade her. But she is now in a state of constant denial, and on one level, she really does not know the truth, she will not accept it, and instead she twists it to fit her warped ideas. It is part of Evelyn's inability and unwillingness to face painful facts and to insist instead on a fantasy version of reality that is ultimately so dangerous.

Evelyn's behavior becomes more violent, her aggression becomes unleashed, and the destructive, rather than the more tender nature, of her love for Dave is revealed. She begins to stalk him. In the throes of her obsession, Evelyn seems to have no capacity for guilt, remorse, or empathy for the man she is persecuting with her insane passion. She is blind to the differences between loving feelings, however intense, and an obsessive need to possess, control, and eventually destroy the other. Evelyn is prepared to get rid of anyone standing in her way, including

Dave himself and the more rational parts of her own psyche, even to the point of staging a suicide attempt.

Evelyn's wish to destroy Dave's girlfriend Tobie reflects her need to destroy any obstruction in her way. She now has given up all need to reflect and understand the nature of reality because this would force her to feel concern about what she is doing to others.

At the root of Evelyn's psychopathology is an idealization of masculine power, aggression, and destructiveness that overcomes the more feminine qualities of compassion and containment, here denigrated and seen as signs of weakness. Much of the film's shock appeal resides in seeing such unbridled aggression so clearly located in the female character. It perpetuates the myth of the dangerous phallic woman who will devour and castrate in order to satisfy her own desires. The film effectively represents the characteristics of the stalking behavior, predating a considered recognition of this disorder, and the vulnerability of public figures at the receiving end of it. It shows with sensitivity how a stalker's own helplessness and anguish can be projected onto the victim.

Another aspect that makes the film so effective is that it touches on people's repressed sexual and aggressive fantasies. There has been much written on the concept of women loving too much. The movie also touches on two particularly complex issues. First is that the relationship between persecutors and victims can sometimes be less straightforward than it looks. Those who have researched the phenomenon of bullying, for instance, have identified the part played, often unconsciously, by those who endure it. Without implying that abusive behavior of any kind is justifiable, it is nonetheless important, if we want to understand it, to identify the possible presence of collusive components.

The second issue concerns the realization that the boundaries between external and inner realities, between fact and imagination, can be ill defined, sometimes to the point of psychosis. Evelyn just couldn't tell the difference between the two states—a confusion that led to an ultimately fatal confrontation.

Interestingly enough, on first reading the script of *Play Misty for Me,* Eastwood recalled an incident in his youth when an older woman became obsessed with him, threatening suicide when he tried to end the liaison. In the part of Dave, Eastwood shifted his screen persona from arch-male chauvinist to that of a helpless, confused, anguished, distraught, and phallically endangered man.

Fatal Attraction

Another well-known film that deals with women exploiting and stalking men is Adrian Lyne's *Fatal Attraction,* released in 1981. In it a very similar storyline is worked out wherein a" one-night" stand results in a woman becoming obsessed with a man who, in this case, is married. After the brief affair, the woman loses all sense of reality and begins to terrorize the man and his family, giving herself completely over to the fantasy that there really is something between them.

Daniel is a successful, happily married attorney living in Manhattan with his wife and daughter when he meets Alex, a book editor, at a business party one night when his wife and daughter are out of town for the weekend. Daniel has a one-night fling with Alex.

Alex's mental instability surfaces when she attempts suicide after Daniel rebuffs her attempts to continue the liaison. Daniel thinks the affair is forgotten, but Alex shows up at various places to see him. She waits at his office one day to apologize and invite him to the opera, *Madame Butterfly,* but he turns her down. She then calls Daniel's office repeatedly until he tells his secretary that he will not take her calls. Alex then calls Daniel's home at all hours and informs him that she is pregnant and plans to keep the baby. Although Daniel wants nothing to do with her, she argues that he must take responsibility. Alex shows up at Daniel's apartment (which is for sale) and meets his wife, Beth, feigning interest as a buyer. Later that night, Daniel goes to Alex's apartment to confront her about her actions.

In response, she replies, "Well, what am I supposed to do? You won't answer my calls, you change your number, I'm not going to be *ignored,* Daniel!"

Daniel moves his family to the upstate village of Bedford, but this doesn't deter Alex. She has a tape recording delivered to Daniel filled with verbal abuse. She stalks him in a parking garage, pours acid on his vehicle, and follows him home one night to spy on him, Beth, and their daughter Ellen from the bushes in their yard. The sight of the happy family life literally makes her sick to her stomach. Alex's obsession eventually turns into madness. Daniel approaches the police to apply for a restraining order against Alex (claiming that it is for a client), but the police lieutenant says that he cannot violate Alex's rights without probable cause and that the adulterer has to own up to his adultery.

Alex's rage eventually escalates into madness, slowly exposing her severe mental disorder.

At one point, while the family is away from home, Alex kills Ellen's pet rabbit and puts it on their stove to boil. After this Daniel tells Beth of the affair and Alex's pregnancy. Beth is infuriated asks and him to leave. Before he goes Daniel calls Alex to tell her that Beth knows about the affair. Beth gets on the phone and warns Alex over the phone that if she persists, she will kill her. After this, Alex kidnaps Ellen, the daughter, from school and takes her to an amusement park, buying her ice cream as well as taking her on a roller coaster. Beth begins to search for her daughter, but she is injured in a car accident while in a state of panic. Daniel approaches the police about having Alex arrested, but the police still say they lack cause to take action against her, although they can drive by his residence to watch for intruders. Beth is briefly hospitalized and soon released after which she forgives Daniel and he returns home. Angered by what's happened because of Alex, Daniel barges into her apartment, severely beating her. In his rage, he tries to kill her, but stops, and as he does, Alex turns the tables and tries to kill him with a knife from her kitchen.

Daniel overpowers her but leaves the knife and quits fighting. However, Alex just smiles, clearly deranged, misinterpreting his actions. Alex then decides to eliminate what she sees as her main obstacle: the wife. While Beth is in her bathroom of her house, Alex sneaks in and attacks her with a chef's knife. Daniel hears the screaming and runs in, wrestles Alex into the bathtub, and seemingly drowns her. But then she suddenly emerges from the water, swinging the knife. Beth, who went searching for Daniel's gun, shoots Alex in the chest, killing her. The final scene shows police cars outside Daniel and Beth's house. As Daniel finishes talking with the cops, he walks inside, where his wife is waiting for him. They embrace and proceed upstairs as the camera focuses on a picture on the table of Daniel, Beth, and Ellen.

The story follows in many respects *Play Misty for Me*. Both films deal with that fact that the blurring of external and inner realities between fact and imagination can be ill defined, as is the case in psychotic conditions. Evelyn and Alex just couldn't tell the difference between what they felt they must have and what they reasonably could take for themselves. Their exploitation emerges from severe personality disorders as their emotional energies became totally bound up in these dynamics. The following film is, if possible, an even more terrifying depiction of this state of mind—not one of stalking but one where the need to control the man is overriding.

Misery

This 1990 film does not involve sex as much as a more complicated notion of control. The female stalker in this film displays different dynamics than the antagonists in the other two films. In fact, *Misery* offers a more complex depiction of the male who is being terrorized and illustrates what is happening to him. The previous two films portray the male as a sexual victim, while in *Misery* the plot has to do with controlling the male to the point of hacking his body parts off piece by piece.

Famed novelist Paul Sheldon is the author of romance novels involving the character Misery Chastaine. After finishing his latest novel, he departs from Silver Creek, Colorado, to New York. In a blizzard, his car goes off the road. He is rescued by Annie Wilkes and brought to her home.

Both of Paul's legs are broken, and he has a dislocated shoulder, leaving him bedridden and largely unable to move. Annie claims she is his number one fan and goes on and on about how she cherishes Paul and his novels. Annie initially seems to be a kind nurse with a happy-go-lucky attitude that hides the fact that she is mentally disturbed. Paul lets her read one of his newest novels. She objects to the profanity; while she is feeding him, she loses her balance, spilling some soup on him, but regains control and apologizes calmly.

Annie then gets a copy of Paul's latest book, *Misery's Child*, the last Misery novel, as Paul has decided to write other stories, including the one he has already finished. When she gets to the section where Paul has Misery killed off, she goes into a rage, having an intense need for Misery to continue to live in Paul's novels. She then tells him that she never contacted the hospital about his condition nor anyone Paul knows. When Annie leaves the house to run errands, Paul decides to escape but finds she has locked the door. The next morning, Annie makes Paul burn his latest novel. He initially refuses until Annie starts pouring gas onto the bedspread, making it clear that she will set the bed on fire if he doesn't comply. Annie can't entertain the idea that Paul will put an end to Misery in his novel.

Planning another escape, Paul stashes some pills that Annie had hoped to drug him. In the meantime, Annie makes him write a Misery novel entitled *Misery's Return,* in which he brings the character back to

153

life. As Annie is setting up a typewriter, Paul spots a hairpin on the floor that he thinks he can use to unlock his door. He sends Annie into town to get him typewriter paper. While she is away, Paul unlocks his door but then sees that both doors out of the house are locked tight.

When Paul has satisfied Annie with his work on resurrecting Misery, he asks her if she will have dinner with him, and she happily accepts. As they dine in his room, Paul manages to drug her wine, but his plot is foiled when Annie accidentally knocks over the candle and spills the drugged wine.

Later Paul finds newspaper clippings about his presumed death and Annie's past, in which she was convicted in the multiple murders of infants. One night Annie is carrying a handgun when she comes to give Paul his medicine. Paul gets a butcher knife from the kitchen to defend himself. In the middle of the night, Annie drugs Paul and the following morning ties him up and tells him that she knows he has left his room in her absence and that she has found out that he plans to kill her. In a brutally shocking scene, she then breaks his ankles with a sledgehammer.

In the meantime, the local sheriff, Buster, has been investigating Paul's disappearance. He comes across an article with Annie in it and reads about her love for the Misery books. At a visit to the general store, Buster discovers that Annie has been buying typing paper. Buster becomes very curious and visits Annie, who by this time has hidden Paul in the basement. Buster inspects the house but finds nothing. As Buster leaves, Paul regains consciousness and tries to get Buster's attention. Buster finds Paul in the basement but is shot and killed by Annie.

Distraught, Annie decides to end both her and Paul's lives, but Paul talks her out of it by convincing her that he loves her and that the novel needs to be finished. He also secretly obtains some lighter fluid, planning to set the book on fire.

As Paul finishes the last chapter, he tells Annie to get a cigarette with a match and a glass of champagne. As he sends her to get a second glass, he drenches the book with lighter fluid. When she returns, he sets the book on fire; as she tries to put the fire out, he bashes her in the head with the typewriter. A brawl breaks out between them with Paul getting the upper hand. He trips her, causing her to land headfirst on the typewriter. As Paul escapes his room, Annie lunges on top of him, but he is able to bash her in the head again with a small steel pig statue, killing her.

Eighteen months later Paul (now able to walk again) meets with his publishing agent in a restaurant, discussing his first non-Misery novel called *The Higher Education of J. Philip Stone*, which has become a real success. His agent asks if he wants to write a nonfiction book about his time with Annie, but Paul claims it would not be good for him. He then sees a vision of Annie as a waitress, but it turns out to be someone else. The waitress claims that she is his number one fan, to which Paul responds, "That's very sweet of you." A frightening ending.

Psychology of the Film

Misery teases out a very complicated relationship between Paul and Annie and his nightmarish experiences with a woman who is attempting to control, if not infantilize, him. What might be less obvious and more interesting is that Paul's terror of Annie may disguise a desire on an unconscious level to return to the controlling mother, to regress to a pleasurable state of total dependency and reliance upon the mother to fulfill his every need.

The film is adapted from Stephen King's masochistic fantasy, a nightmare of the male body emasculated, the male psyche stripped of its independence. The man flirts with the idea of total dependency and vulnerability. Paul must master his fear of weakness to prove his manhood in an act of sadistic triumph over a female body. King probes the male unconscious and conjures up images of women as feminine monsters, such as witches and vampires, that haunt the male's childish fantasies.

These fantasies repel but also enlighten, as they represent the dark side of the male's unconscious, particularly the deep-seated attitude of extreme ambivalence to the mother who nurtures but who also has the power to torment and infantilize. In this light, Paul's vision of Annie symbolizes the fear of the devouring mother—the mother who will destroy the child who represents this overpowering, engulfing force.

Annie is then acting out the worst fears of a boy with a horror of an overpowering mother. But Annie is more than just a boy's fantasy as it finds new life in adult form. Annie is the phallic mother par excellence. She is the devouring mother—a strange combination of love and disapproval, overindulgence and punishment. Ironically, the horrifying incident makes Paul into a real writer, one who writes as if his life depends on it. He becomes more individuated as a man; overcoming the horror of Annie is actually empowering as Paul is able to use his phallic strength in the climax of the film to triumph over her. He must destroy the dependent female within him to realize his independence. As he writes in his fictionalized version of the story, "To get out of this, he would have to kill her," which essentially means that he must separate from her.

Annie becomes the mother who wants to live through the child's creativity and stifles his development to manhood. She must make sure she can control Paul and hurt him if he disobeys. Annie is unlike the two previous exploiters: They represent a woman's vengeance when being rejected by the man, and they misconstrue the relationship because of an emotional pathology. Annie, on the other hand, takes the place of a feared and destructive mother figure who crosses boundaries and who knows no limits as to what she can rightfully do.

All three films highlight what could be called the "craving personality." The three women who were portrayed had no firm sense of themselves. They are clinging and desperate with a strong need for actual physical proximity. They did not exist outside the realities of the relationships they had conjured up in their minds.

Less Destructive Stalkers

A recent film, *Tabloid* (2011), tells the true story of Joyce McKinney who, in 1977, was involved in an affair known as *The Case of the Manacled Mormon*, which was made to order for the British tabloids. A former Miss Wyoming, McKinney was alleged to have kidnapped an American Mormon missionary in London, handcuffed him to a bed, and made him a sex slave. When caught, she claimed that she was intervening to rescue him from a cult.

The story began when McKinney fell in love with a nondescript Mormon named Kirk Anderson, who claimed to reciprocate her affection. However, before they could be married, he left on a missionary trip to the United Kingdom. Joyce caught up with him there and kidnapped him. They spent three days together in an isolated cabin having sex. He escaped, and she was tried but jumped bail and fled to the United States before being sentenced.

In the film, Joyce explains her actions by saying she did it for love and that the sex was consensual. In her telling of the events, there is an abundance of humor, and her story could be seen as a comedy. She never wanted to hurt her beloved but could not get over being jilted. The sensational story served as fodder for lots of lurid newspaper headlines in Great Britain for much of 1977. To this day, Joyce affirms that she never did anything wrong. In fact, she eagerly cooperated in the making of the film by Errol Morris. This real-life account is in stark contrast to the villainous, destructive attitude of the other three films.

The story is also reminiscent of the measures Monica Lewinsky took to try and gain the affections of President Bill Clinton in the late 1990s. Columnist Maureen Dowd has noted the fine line between trapping and stalking. "In old movies," she writes, "girls would have to do shoe-leather investigating if they wanted to be romantic gumshoes." Monica stationed herself in flashy dresses and her trademark black beret while waiting on rope lines and in the path of the presidential motorcade. She also studied her prey's preferences "and bought them for him, enticing him further in her premeditated stalking safari" (*New York Times*, 7/14/2006, p. 23).

Sidney Blumenthal, a noted journalist regarded Lewinsky as an unbalanced stalker and testified to a grand jury that Monica had told him, "They call me the stalker...If I can say we had an affair, they won't call me that."

Maureen Dowd contrasts some feminists who have characterized Lewinsky as a "slutty stalker" with others who believed that Lewinsky had gotten a bum rap as she was stereotyped as a woman who "had it coming to her if she flirted, wore a short skirt or liked sex."

Feminist Katha Pollitt confessed, in a article in *The New Yorker*, that after her lover left her, "I was like Javert [the obsessed inspector in *Les Miserables*], hunting him through the sewers of cyberspace, moving from link to link in the dark, like Spider-Man flinging himself by a filament over the shadowy chasm between one roof and another."

In the throes of romantic love, Dr. Helen Fisher of Rutgers University says that some people when rejected contemplate stalking, homicide, or even suicide. The drive for romantic love and union can be stronger than the will to live.

Femme Fatales

A femme fatale is a mysterious and seductive woman whose charms are aimed to ensnare her lovers in bonds of irresistible desire, often leading them into compromising, dangerous, and deadly situations. Stories of their ability to entrance and hypnotize their victims with a spell were, in their earliest incarnations, seen as being literally supernatural; hence, the femme fatale today is still often described as having a power akin to an enchantress, vampire, witch, or demon.

The femme fatale tortures her lover with inconsistent confirmations of her affection. She has the power to drive her lover to the point of obsession and exhaustion so that he is incapable of making rational decisions. During the film noir era of the 1940s and 1950s, the femme fatale flourished in American cinema. An early example was 1941's *The Maltese Falcon,* where the actress Mary Astor played a character Brigid O'Shaughnessy, who uses her skills to murder Sam Spade's partner. Barbara Stanwyck plays a femme fatale in *Double Indemnity* and seduces a hapless insurance salesman and persuades him to kill her husband.

The femme fatale has generated divergent opinions among social scholars. Some believe that they are really examples of female independence and a threat to traditional female gender roles—that they express women's ancient and eternal control of the sexual realm.

The femme fatale of the film noir movies of the 1940s and 1950s is representative of several personality disorders characterized by histrionics, self-absorption, and psychopathology. It may be no accident that the overabundance of films exhibiting the femme fatale coincided with female acquisition of economic and social clout in real life. In fact, film noir movies can be seen resulting from the alteration of World War II-era American culture, symbolizing the female threat to the status quo. These women were a composite of power, lust, and greed.

The film noir can be identified by its cynical, nihilistic view of the world. Vice, licentiousness, wrongdoing, and impulsive behavior are all portrayed in a manner and style more realistic than Hollywood had ever attempted before. These femme fatales in these films represented a concerted attempt by American filmmakers to depict women in a genuine, if somewhat harsh way. They could be just as sexually voracious and as potentially murderous as any man and just as susceptible to corruption and greed.

Feminist authors have viewed film noir femme fatales as energized, intelligent, and able to elicit strength from their sexuality—attributes that have usually been reserved for men. It is not the eventual destruction of these women that we remember as much as their potency, drive, and compelling ability to manipulate men through the power of their sexuality. These domineering women, castrating types, and unfaithful wives seemed to personify the worst of a male sexual fantasy.

Remember, in World War II the emergence of "Rosie the Riveter" reflected a pervasive frustration with women's traditional gender assignments and their search for even limited amounts of autonomy and self-reliance. The place of women in society was transformed forever.

However, in this new role, women were portrayed in a critical and disparaging way. They evolved on screen as evil, duplicitous vixens, sexually powerful and poisonous to the male.

These women represent the ultimate misogynistic, dystopic fantasy. They control their own sexuality and use it to gain power over the male. They fly in the face of the general attitude toward women as finding contentment by fulfilling the roles of housewife and mother. At the conclusion of the Second World War, when returning veterans were granted preference in employment, many women lost their foothold on cultural power. By 1947 three million women had resigned or been fired from their positions. It is no wonder that feminists suggest that the film noir stands as the only period in American film in which women are deadly but sexy, exciting and strong. These are not "fallen women" victimized by patriarchal exploitation but rather ambitious exploiters whose misdeeds merit punishment.

The narcissism of these fatal women is demonstrated as they often gaze at their own images in the mirror. They are totally self-absorbed. In the final scene of *The Lady from Shanghai* (1948), Elsa Bannister (Rita Hayworth) is confronted by her adversary, actually her husband in the form of endless reflections of her in the mirror at an amusement park fun house. As the mirror shatters by bullets fired from her husband, the shards reveal the many faces of this femme fatale; in some of the mirrored panels, her appearance changes from looking strong and self-confident to weak and vulnerable in others. We in the audience are in a position to view all of these aspects of her personality so that the shot elicits both a literal (physical) point of view and a figurative (emotional) one as well.

In *Double Indemnity*, Barbara Stanwyck portrays the archetypal femme fatale. She represents a self-centered denial of motherhood and a pervasive narcissism. She is a monstrous castrator, exuding charm under pressure, demonstrating control and self-possession. She demonstrates a range of vicious, calculating acts.

Early in the film, she seduces Walter, an insurance salesman, and manipulates him into murdering her husband after insuring his life with a double indemnity clause. She proceeds to coldly participate in the killing, and we later discover that she had poisoned her husband's first wife. When complications in her scheme develop, she tries to murder

Walter. Toward the end of the movie, we learn that she has been having an affair with her stepdaughter's fiancé while this whole chain of events has been unfolding.

After murdering her husband, she emerges as the phallic woman who seeks to usurp male authority in her desire for money and for the destruction of the family. Yet in the end, she just isn't able to pull off the whole pretense. She is unable to fire the fatal shot in the climactic scene, showing that she is unable to live up to her own phallic desires. She is made vulnerable through lust and passion, that is, through her nature as a woman.

On the other hand, Walter's comparative potency is callously demonstrated by the ease with which he can pull the trigger on her. But not before she shoots and most likely kills him.

These fatal women are both a representation of some aspects of the larger American culture and create a certain style and personality for women in this era. These cinema seductresses, with the potency and strength to annihilate men, may in some ways be viewed as overdrawn, cynical precursors of the potential of women to exploit.

It's not totally a man's world anymore.

All About Eve

This is a film that deals with a different kind of exploitation. It is a story of a woman who schemes to get ahead and who subtly works out her life to damage people who stand in her way. However, in this process she makes sure that she is appreciated and trusted and then she can sting like a wasp. She is patient and well versed in interpersonal skills, and so she can play upon other's foibles. She sees vulnerabilities and strikes as if she were stalking her prey with a deadly venom. She doesn't commit fraud or cheat her clients, as did Madoff, and she doesn't leave such destruction in her path, but oddly enough there are similarities that I will attempt to spell out.

The film begins at an awards dinner, where the newest and brightest star on Broadway, Eve Harrington, is being presented with the Sarah Siddons Award for her breakout performance as Cora in *Footsteps on the Ceiling*. The droll newspaper critic Addison DeWitt observes the proceedings and, in a sardonic voice-over, recalls how Eve's star rose as quickly as it did.

The film flashes back a year. Margo Channing is one of the biggest stars on Broadway, but despite her unmatched success, she is beginning to show her age. After a performance one night, Margo's close friend

Karen Richards, the wife of the play's author, Lloyd Richards, meets a besotted fan, Eve Harrington, in the cold alley outside the stage door. Recognizing her from standing room (Eve claims to have seen every performance), Karen takes her backstage to meet Margo. Eve claims to be Margo's biggest fan, who tells the group gathered in Margo's dressing room—Karen and Lloyd, Margo's lover Bill Sampson, and Margo's maid Birdie—that she followed Margo's theatrical tour to New York after seeing her in a play in San Francisco. Margo is impressed and quickly befriends Eve, who willingly offers to assist Margo in small ways. Margo soon offers Eve a job as assistant, leaving Birdie, who dislikes Eve, feeling put out.

Eve begins working to supplant Margo, scheming to become her understudy, and tricks Karen into sabotaging Margo's car while she is in Connecticut so that she will be forced to miss a performance. Eve, knowing in advance she will be asked to go on, invites the city's theater critics to the theater that night so that they will get to see her in the role. The night is a triumph. Eve makes a pass at Bill, but he rejects her. She then schemes to secure the role of Cora in Bill's latest play, despite the fact that Lloyd has written this new character for Margo. She then threatens Karen, telling her that she will expose how she sabotaged Margo's car unless she can get the role of Cora. Before she can put this plan in action, however, Margo announces to everyone's surprise that she does not wish to play Cora and would prefer to continue in her current play and would even be willing to take it on tour. Eve secures the role and attempts to climb higher by enlisting the help of the theater critic Addison DeWitt. Just before the out-of-town opening of her play, Eve faces DeWitt with her next plan—to marry Lloyd after he divorces his wife, a sheer delusion of hers. DeWitt is infuriated that Eve has used him and reveals that he knows all about her. He blackmails her, forcing her to become his mistress in exchange for his silence.

Eve becomes a Broadway star and is presented with an award for her performance in the role of Cora. She arrives home and encounters an apparently besotted young fan named Phoebe who has sneaked into her apartment. Phoebe begins to attend to Eve's needs. Phoebe answers the door to Addison who has returned with Eve's forgotten award. While Eve rests in the other room, Phoebe tries on Eve's gown and poses in front of the mirror with her award. Phoebe steps up to the mirrors, which are transformed to reveal thousands of images of herself.

The story of *All About Eve* originated in an anecdote related to Mary Orr by actress Elisabeth Bergner. While performing in *The Two Mrs. Carrolls* during 1943 and 1944, Bergner allowed a young fan to become part of her household and employed her as an assistant but later regretted her generosity when the woman attempted to undermine her. Referring to her only as "the terrible girl," Bergner related the events to Orr, who used it as the basis for her short story "The Wisdom of Eve." In the story, Orr depicts the girl as a more ruthless character and allows her to succeed in stealing the career of the older actress. Bergner later confirmed the basis of the story in her autobiography *Bewundert viel, und viel gescholten (Greatly Admired, and Greatly Scolded)*.

Eve the Exploiter

The plot of the film has been used numerous times (frequently as an outright homage to the film), with one famous example being a 1974 episode of *The Mary Tyler Moore Show*, "A New Sue Ann." In the episode, the character of Sue Ann Nivens, hostess of a popular local cooking show, hires a young, pretty, and very eager fan as her apprentice and assistant, but the neophyte quickly begins to sabotage her mentor in an attempt to replace her as host of the show. (Sue Ann, however, unlike Margo Channing, prevails in the end, countering the young woman's attempts to steal her success and sending her on her way.)

There is a personality type in the psychological nomenclature that is referred to as an *as-if* type. Eve Harrington demonstrates the pathology of the *as-if personality*. She schemes and exploits the friendship and support that Margo Channing has given her. As the story unfolds, we begin to see different, more complex parts of Eve, and then we come to understand more clearly as the plot evolves what she is attempting to do with the friendship of those people around her and how she manipulates and conspires in the destruction of the lives of others in the ruthless pursuit of realizing her ambitions. We get the impression that her whole relationship to life is without any genuine concern for the other yet outwardly runs along *as if* it were complete. She has good intelligence, displays well-ordered emotional expressiveness, is quite talented, and impresses others as establishing an intense, loving, friendly, and sympathetic relationship. However, as the movie unfolds, we see another side of her—something even deceitful, underhanded—much different from our initial impression.

The other side that is initially concealed contains much hostility, a lack of appropriate emotional response, and a defective moral structure.

From the literature of as-if personalities, we see that it characterizes the behavior of many individuals in the arts, in politics, and in the world of drama. The profession of acting seems to attract as-if personalities. Actors are people in need of constant narcissistic supplies. In acting there is a concealment of the true self. The actors play at what they might have been. The prevailing motivations in actors are attempts to relieve anxiety, to seduce and overpower the audience, and to master the external world, like children at play. So we might ask again, "What is wrong with Eve? What is she up to?" And yet at the same time she is so stimulating, amusing, attractive, and interesting.

The first impression we get of Eve is that she is just lovely. She is concerned with others and what they are going through. Her relationships are serious and bear all the earmarks of friendship, love, sympathy, and understanding; but soon the viewer perceives something strange and raises the question that is hard to put one's finger on. As the film develops, it becomes clear that all of her relationships are devoid of any trace of warmth, that all the expressions of emotion are formal, that all inner experience is completely excluded. It resembles the performance of the actor who is technically well trained but who lacks the necessary spark to make his or her impersonations true to life. So outwardly at least, Eve conducts her life as if she possessed a complete and sensitive emotional capacity. She is not the person who exhibits a coldness of a repressed person. In these conditions there very well may be a deeper emotional life hidden behind a wall. No, in the as-if personality, Eve needs to reach out to the world in an effort to avoid an underlying anxiety about herself, with a readiness to pick up signals from the outer world and to mold herself and her behavior accordingly.

At first, Eve's love, friendship, and attachment has something very rewarding for Margo. She seems to be the quintessence of devotion, always there for her, the consummate friend and helper. But we see soon enough that she really lacks real concern and instead brings an emptiness and dullness to the emotional atmosphere. But as soon as the former people in her life are discarded or they discard her, she exchanges them for new ones and the process is repeated.

A similar emptiness that is so evident in her emotional life appears also in her moral structure. Completely without character, wholly unprincipled, her morals, her ideals, and her convictions can get swept under the rug with ease. Her overenthusiastic adherence to Margo can be quickly and completely replaced by another one without the slightest trace of remorse. And we see underneath it all aggressive tendencies that earlier are masked by devotion. Odd though, as adept as she is in reading others and their motivations, she becomes utterly obtuse to many ordinary considerations, like thinking she will marry Lloyd or that Addison DeWitt will want nothing from her after she enlists him to advance her career.

What we begin to find is that once the cohesive side of Eve's as-if personality fades and is given up temporarily, an amazingly crude and poorly knit one emerges. This is the earlier side to her. It would have been too hard for her to sustain this role without the emotional support from someone who especially believes in and nourishes it, namely Karen.

Eve seems to be repeatedly seeking conformation about who she in order to overcome her sense of incompleteness. This may well be the secret of her appeal to others and maybe explains why others are taken in. In this story, another interesting set of dynamics emerge. Margo is an aging actress and could be old enough to be Eve's mother. So Eve may be living out an oedipal conflict through revival of her earlier discords with her mother. What she is doing could be seen as an aggressive act of displacing the mother. It further serves to give a temporary feeling of completion of her sense of herself that can be more nearly achieved in this way than in her ordinary life. While she is going through this struggle, she feels she has a greater sense of integrity and reality. And this is reinforced and sustained by the awareness that others believe in her and finally by the intoxication of being in the limelight, her final success as an actress. She not only displaces and replaces the mother; she outdoes her and finds great achievement in the process. So in the final analysis, Eve's behavior is an attempt to achieve a sense of reality, completeness, and competence as a woman and to actively surpass the mother—an interesting type of woman to ponder and wonder about. She certainly expands our understanding of the exploiter and the psychological components that bind the 'as if' with the actions of exploitation. She could be related to Madoff they share so much together. In fact, the as-if character resembles the psychopath in many ways.

Chapter Eleven

Wizard of Odds:
How Jack Molinas Attempted to
Corrupt the Game of Basketball

The Ultimate Exploiter

After looking over and analyzing the details, actions, and character of the exploiters, it becomes clear that many of them share common features. There is always intent to harm or hurt another person. They are usually bright people, who seem be in tune with the wishes of their victims, and to some extent they must be sensitive enough in order to deceive successfully. Expert exploiters must be able to intuit others' characters, their interests, their prohibitions, their propensity for guilt, and their anxieties and loyalties. They are very good at influencing other people. One person will be influenced by an appeal to their vanity, another to their hopes of a better future, and yet another to the promise of monies and wonderful riches. The most effective exploitations are accomplished when the deceiver knows and understands the other person well, and this knowledge and understanding is, to a large extent, dependent on a particular kind of empathy.

Exploiters use other people as a means to an end rather than as fellow human beings; they devalue others as people in their own right and see them only as tools. Frequently, the other person is an object of contempt, a disposable item, to be used and discarded or to be kept around for convenience and pleasure but not for friendship. It is true that people can exploit their friends, but while they are engaged in the exploitation, the quality of the friendship is significantly altered. Exploiters not only derive pleasure from the success of the interaction, they also experience a sense of power and exhilaration.

Almost all exploiters are hyper-ambitious. They strive to win at all costs, and in this pursuit they are willing to break the rules of socially acceptable behavior. The former coach of the Green Bay Packers, Vince Lombardi, was once quoted as saying that "winning is the only thing." There is a sinister connotation to this. The desire to win at all costs is useful when crushing one's foes in warfare. But in everyday life we do not aim to kill our opponents. Spying is acceptable wartime behavior— in World War II the Allies had to deceive the Axis forces when planning the Normandy invasion. We were all were impressed by the tactics that were employed. When such tactics are used by corporations or individuals, however, we are not so impressed.

Exploiters follow their own rules, and often what is legal or illegal is of little concern to them. Lombardi, the coach of the Green Bay Packers also added, "Winning isn't everything; it's the only thing." This suggests some fanatic passion to prevail and triumph. Little children, one observes, do not play, as adults glowingly remember, in carefree innocence, but with bitter and combative intensity. Often children playing games will cheat without compunction. Good sportsmanship is a value that comes with maturity. In a sense the exploiter holds onto a child's vision of winning. So when an exploiter displays these behaviors, he or she is clearly working out some childhood conflict.

Most adults would affirm that they want to win—but in a fair and square fashion. The exploiter has no such scruples. In fact, cheating on exams has become more and more of a problem in universities as attested by many college deans. Students have been known to break into instructors' offices in order to steal tests. In this sense they are exploiting the rules of acceptable college behavior. And when caught at it, these students don't feel bad about what they have done—they feel bad about getting caught.

So now we are confronted with a type of person who not only cheats but also seems to have a compulsion to deceive others. This kind of behavior can be observed when it comes to men cheating on their wives, especially politicians who you would think would be especially concerned about acting in a morally correct fashion. But that statement is really laughable in the present day.

Exploiters possess an excessive amount of greed that takes on the guise of ambition. They want to outwit the other person by whatever means they can employ. Our former president, Richard M. Nixon, didn't lose any sleep over the dishonesty that went on in his administration. He simply tried to lie his way through it.

No one person can represent all the psychological aspects of exploitation—there are too many variations and a multitude of motivations. One man, however, comes close. He was reckless, evil, and just couldn't abide by the rules of the game. Did he have to? Of course not, but he was driven to corrupt the life around him, garnering some special pleasure of feeling as if he beat the system. In beating the system, he brought down everything that he touched. Wherever he put his hands, it was bound to become tainted with the shadiness and dishonesty of his intent.

Jack Molinas

Jack Molinas was one of the greatest basketball players of his day. When only a rookie with the Fort Wayne Pistons, he was already a certified NBA All-Star and an amazingly gifted athlete. In addition, he was an Ivy League graduate with a genius-level IQ. He had lots of money, and he was handsome, charismatic, and stood six feet six inches tall. With his sweet, buoyant smile, Molinas was irresistible to women, although he did not treat them all that nicely.

But despite possessing an abundance of God-given gifts, Molinas also had a flair for larceny and would much rather swindle somebody than earn an honest dollar. For Jack Molinas, the real sport was in exploiting the other guy while playing the game of basketball. Starting early in life, he consorted with gamblers to fix ball games in high school, college, and in professional basketball. Molinas was so well schooled in manipulating people that he was able to enlist many other players in fixing games.

This was a risky dodge, yet the prospect of facing jail time if he was caught did not seem to trouble Molinas; he felt invulnerable and was confident that he could always think or talk his way out of any predicament.

In his time, Molinas was a world-class athlete, a lawyer, and a master of the stock market, but he was also a big-time gambler and fixer in league with the Mafia, a double- and triple-crosser, a jailbird, a pornographer, and a loan shark.

A defining dynamic of many corrupt exploiters is that they live on the edge—disaster is always a heartbeat away. As terrifying as this prospect would be for most of us, exploiters wouldn't have it any other way. They just can't play it safe—they must live their lives as if they are teetering at the edge of a cliff. Obviously, this arouses massive amounts of tension and excitement. It must become addictive because they reenact the same kind of scenarios over and over again.

Taking another look at Molinas—his manipulation and cheating started as far back as high school in New York City. Molinas attended Stuyvesant, a school for the best and the brightest. He was also a gifted athlete. In fact, his extraordinary talent for playing basketball enabled his school to get into the finals of the PSAL high school championship.

The scene now shifts to the championship game where Stuyvesant squared off against a very tough squad from Lincoln High School. The game was rated a virtual toss-up by the oddsmakers—Stuyvesant was a one- or two-point favorite. Molinas was awesome at the start of the game and carried Stuyvesant. However, after Stuyvesant gained the upper hand, the game started to change—Molinas played small. The Lincoln players took the ball from him again and again. Molinas played slow: Lincoln players went by and around him. Stuyvesant's star player seemed to have lost interest in the game. Molinas didn't want to shoot, and so he just passed the ball when it was thrown to him. With thirty seconds left in the game, Molinas went to the foul line for a shot that could tie the game. He missed by a mile, and Lincoln ran out the clock.

As Molinas was leaving the court, he spotted a schoolmate named Red, a friend and ardent supporter who looked up to Molinas as his hero. Red couldn't look Molinas in the eye. It was obvious that Molinas had thrown the game.

How can we understand Molinas's motivation? It was the biggest high school game of the year and one that Molinas could have won; yet he preferred to throw the game. Could it have been for the money? Molinas, even at that young age, was betting on many other sporting events, for instance Sandy Koufax pitching for the Dodgers. Something must have been deeply ingrained in his psyche to allow him to corrupt the sport he loved and to cheat the fans, his coach, and the team. Perhaps it was a need to spit in everyone's eye. Did having the power to affect the outcome of the game by underhanded means give him such a sense of superiority?

Whatever demons motivated him, Molinas would carry on with these illegal activities for the rest of his life, consequences be damned— the signature behavioral trait of the exploiter.

Molinas came from a comfortable family. As a child he always had money; he was the richest guy in the park. But he had to gamble, and he had to win. Molinas was hardwired to do things in a devious way even when the ends he desired could have been achieved just as effectively by honest means.

His big speech he once gave to a friend was this: "I can con the world; I can bullshit the world; I can connive the world; I'm brighter than you guys; I can steal; I can manipulate; I'll always get another chance. If I get caught, I'll get out of it—my father deals with cops all the time."

Molinas played three games at once. There was the game of basketball, which he loved with as much intensity and depth as anything in his life. There was the betting game. And finally there was the game of control in which he played the conflicting roles of the star for one team and the mastermind working out the point spread. He saw himself as a kind of creative artist, composer and performer, taking enormous risks and fearing no reprisal.

Remember, it is one thing to go out on the court and try your best to win. It's another thing to go out on the court and play as well as you can while keeping in mind the point spread so as to win or lose by a certain point margin. It heightens the stakes of the game. For Molinas this is where the action was. He wanted to win the bet, and it didn't really matter if he won the game or not. It is the logic of someone who feels outside the system, who plays by his own rules, who is so self-centered that losing the game rolls off him like water off a log. And worst of all, he rationalized his actions to the point where he saw nothing wrong with his behavior. "What are they doing for me? I play hard and what do I get in return?" We could imagine that this was the way he constructed and defined all situations.

For most athletes, pride in their talent and the adulation it inspires— and, yes, a hefty paycheck—are rewards enough. Not for Molinas. It was all about money—the other stuff was for suckers. Somewhere in his growth process he never acquired the moral compass that guides most of us. Exploiters like Molinas employ a completely different logic—the same logic that permeated the behavior of the executives and traders at Enron; a form of cheating that drove Madoff further and further into his Ponzi scheme; the logic that prompted Irving to lie about his biography of Howard Hughes; that allowed Hunt's deceit and Abramoff's thieving.

Most of these exploiters could have done quite well playing by the rules. But the rules bothered them; they interfered in their aims.

Maybe they felt that abiding by them put them on par with the rest of the plebian human race. Exploiters need to stand out from the rest of the crowd. They play not only to win, but also to prove their superiority over the other guy. Who cares if an act is illegal or illicit—they have granted themselves special dispensations. They are the blessed ones, the special ones. They have anointed themselves to play by their own rules. Given free rein they account for a lot of ruined lives and destroyed reputations and have caused a general erosion of trust that society has in its institutions. Nixon's behavior caused a decline in confidence in our government that continues to this day.

Let's move forward with the story of the infamous career of Molinas whose actions all but destroyed the game of basketball.

Game fixing in high school was just the start of his crooked career: he continued the practice through Columbia University and into professional basketball when he played for the Fort Wayne Zollners, now called the Detroit Pistons in the NBA.

He was caught betting on games while playing for that team, and then officials noticed unnatural fluctuations in the betting line. Two inferences could be drawn: One was that big money was being bet on games involving Fort Wayne. The other was that inside information about the team was leaking out. When they investigated further, they found that Molinas was betting on his team. Initially he shrugged it off; he thought that he would escape punishment by copping a plea and be reinstated. Molinas felt that he would do OK when Commissioner Maurice Podoloff confronted him.

But the commissioner looked Molinas in the eye: "Jack, you're through with basketball."

Molinas heard it, but he didn't believe it.

Podoloff went on: "As least as far as the NBA is concerned. We're in a bad way, Jack. Our whole future is on the line. The league lacks credibility with the public. It's not going over as entertainment, and we've got to maintain these television contracts. The current rules don't allow for the game to be seen at its best, and we're hunting for ways to fix that."

"What's this to do with me?" Molinas asked.

"Now what does this have to do with you, Jack? Well, a report has been made that certain activities have been uncovered, you have admitted them, and it will be made public. Your contract as well as all league contracts specify an interdiction of gambling activities and associations."

Molinas became increasingly frightened as Podoloff continued: "You've admitted to betting on games. Isn't it right?"

Molinas: "Yes, sir."

Podoloff : "Why did you do that?"

Molinas: "Do you want me to admit it? Is that what you want?"

Podoloff: "No, I mean, why did you bet?"

Molinas: "I didn't think it was wrong, as long as I was betting on my own team to win, and as long as no one knew about it."

Podoloff: "Others had to know about it."

Molinas: "Like who?"

Podoloff : "Well, your friend in the Bronx through whom you placed the bets knew. And whoever accepted those bets knew. Don't you see? You were not only doing something illegal; you were providing information that could be used illegally by others."

Molinas's reply was so convoluted that if he had thought about it he would have been embarrassed by it.

Molinas: "I just didn't think about that, sir. I didn't think it was a serious thing. It certainly wasn't serious money. And I thought it was common practice among the pros, that that was one of the big differences from college ball. I was wondering if you had decided to make an example of me, and I wondered why."

Podoloff : "You're an example for young people. Every player is. But so far as the league is concerned you are an individual player who has violated his contract and broken a basic tenet of the league. Any individual player who perpetrates that violation will be dealt with in the same way. There can be no compromise of that tenet. As of now you are the only individual player we know of who has actively compromised it or the league's integrity."

Molinas, hoping to get himself out of trouble, asked the commissioner if he should reveal the names of other players who had been involved in similar gambling activities in exchange for reinstatement.

Podoloff replied that yes, he should tell him about other crooked players but that there would be no deals. Podoloff then said he needed other information—for example, whether Molinas had ever deliberately tried to lose a basketball game. Molinas said that he never threw a game in the NBA or at Columbia or at Stuyvesant.

Podoloff: "Have you ever tried to hold down a score, control the margin of victory?"

Molinas: "No."

Podoloff: "Do you know anyone—a player, a coach, an official, a gambler—who has been involved in any such activity?"

Molinas: "Not that I know of."

Podoloff: "When you were a sophomore at Columbia and you heard about the college scandals, how did you react?"

Molinas: "I was shocked. I didn't know any of the guys involved, never played with them—or against them—but I just couldn't imagine how they could do it...They would have to have no self-respect or regard for others. And besides, a team sport is a team sport, no individual can control the results" (Rosen, C. *The Wizard of Odds: How Jack Molinas Almost Destroyed the Game of Basketball*, 2002).

What is so interesting about this give-and-take was Molinas's brazen gall. He acted the part of an innocent lad. Molinas mentioned that he bet on a few games and then only for his team to win. Yet we know that he had been throwing games as far back as high school, not just for his team to win but also to lose. In fact, he threw that championship game in high school. Molinas was completely at ease when affirming that he didn't realize he was breaking any law.

All we can assume is that this was a man who was born with maybe a small amount of guilt—the emotion that keeps us all in line. It's the feeling that kept Hamlet back from killing his uncle, the nagging voice in our head that arouses anxiety when we know we are cheating on our income tax. Without a modicum of guilt we are all potential thieves, murderers, and of course, exploiters.

A leading child psychologist, Jean Piaget, noted that in late childhood, the child begins to develop the concept of "equity" in which moral judgment relates not only to the rules and peer values but also to the whole spectrum of psychological and social conditions surrounding an action. The child begins to have an interest not only in what is done but also in why it is being done and the effect it may have on others. The child starts to develop a conscience or, as Freud has called it, a super ego.

With equity, we are still capable of distorting or omitting the truth—but not for the pleasure of exploiting another person. People with mature consciences are unlikely to exploit. Of course in societies that openly condone exploitation and see nothing wrong with it, as in the case of many third world countries, the individual, seeing such behavior as normalized, would be more prone to exhibit such behavior.

As with the exploiters we have encountered in previous chapters, we must assume that something interfered with their mature development, much like Molinas's conscience. His is the preeminent example of a deficiency of guilt. Molinas not only had no problem with cheating the system and cheating others, and this seems to have provided him with a great deal of gratification. It wasn't enough for Molinas to be an exceptional athlete. His ability to manipulate the outcome of a game not only by scoring points for his team but by covering the point spread made him feel like an artist, a master manipulator, and a daredevil. In some games, he had three players on one team dumping points. He had two star players on the other team primed to go all out, protecting against any counter-fix. And to top it all off, he had the guarantee to control the game because he had bribed the refs.

However, it all caught up with him in 1963 when the district attorney's office caught on to what he was doing. He was tried and convicted of bribing players. A New York State Supreme Court judge gave him consecutive sentences of five to seven-and-a-half years in jail. He was labeled "a master-fixer, a completely immoral person, and the ringleader of groups that corrupted college ballplayers to dump games for money." Prison was his next stop along the downhill road.

One would think that prison time would both depress and frighten him; however, Molinas thrived in prison. His fellow inmates were impressed with his ability to play sports and his uncanny skill for picking stocks. It was a bit odd that he was able to do this from prison. To add to the mix, by this time he had a law degree and could help other inmates with their parole petitions.

After getting out of prison in 1968 after serving only five years of his sentence, he went right back to his old tricks of enlisting players to fix games.

A friend observed that Molinas started each day on a manic high, and as the day went on he just soared higher and higher. Molinas felt so keenly alive that his capacity to juggle more and more scams was intensified. Despite the fact that he'd already been caught and imprisoned, he either believed he'd never get caught again or subconsciously hoped he would be caught and punished. Along the way, he lost the right to practice law. He linked up with the Mafia, borrowed money, gambled without paying up, and generally screwed whomever he wanted. He had started a pornography company, which thrived, and began to borrow money from mobsters to expand it and then engaged in loan shark activity. But such behavior was not consequence-free. He never got around to paying the mobsters back, and it left them feeling cheated. At age forty-one, a bullet to his head ended his life.

By always taking the riskiest path, Molinas had to know that he would eventually make enemies of a lot of dangerous people. But no exploiter can be a hero without seeking a definition of limits and then exceeding them. Exploiter-heroes are the individuals who, by their excesses, test, prove, define, and redefine our systems. They are compelled to live by their own rules, and we learn, by contrast, how the rest of us must live by ours.

Molinas went too far in 1953 and lost his basketball career. He went too far in 1961 and lost his profession and his freedom. He went too far in 1975 and lost his life.

Exploiters have so many different kinds of reasoning that they use to buoy up their behavior. For example, Molinas always felt that he was doing more for the other person, e.g., he felt that he was putting himself out for Columbia University but got little back in return, and therefore his scams were defensible. This is a typical justification of exploiters—they all feel they are putting so much out and therefore feel as if they are being used and not getting enough back in return. For this reason they can rationalize their moral boundaries and make up their own rules.

Exploiters see the world as a diamond mine and have the right—by virtue of their superior intellect and abilities—to plunder. In a sense they are eternal optimists—they see so much in the world that is theirs for the taking. And in this process they need to gain an edge, and of course, that edge is the practice of deceit and often corruption. They never face the evil implications of what they are doing.

The irony inherent in the narratives of all the exploiters I have discussed—except for womanizers and stalkers—is that they could have done very well by playing it straight and being possessed of superior intelligence, ambition, and energy levels. But because of their impaired consciences, they all followed paths that led to their destruction.

But look at Molinas from a different vantage point: along the way, there were so many alternate strategies he could have employed to gain fame and fortune, to stay on the right side of the law, and to steer clear of the mob. Instead, he went out of his way to put his life in jeopardy. Eventually, he was thrown out of the NBA, served a prison term, lost his license to practice as a lawyer, ran up gambling debts, and angered a number of killers and was eventually murdered.

But to a certain extent, all exploiters do this. Every one of them faces a bleak future. Some are serving long prison sentences; some have been released but now are trusted by no one.

There are exceptions: Michael Milken, who came out of jail a wealthy man.

Abramoff waited out his prison term and now is excited about his new life.

So in the end, most exploiters are essentially self-destructive. On some level they know that the course of action they undertake will lead to their demise, yet they continue on their corrupted road. Is it that they cannot think that far ahead? Wouldn't we expect that Irving would have to realize that at some point Howard Hughes would deny the whole plot to write his autobiography and expose his imposturous behavior? If Irving were asked about this, I am sure that he would have some rationalization for what he was doing. He certainly was able to convince himself of this as well as a number of other people. Odd but true.

In an interview with an old friend of Molinas, Barry Storick, an attorney in Charlotte, was asked if he remembered the games at Leon Kaiser Park that took place in New York City.

"Very well," he replied.

"How about the gambling?"

"I was never aware of any of it."

"Did you know that Molinas and some of his friends were betting on games?"

"No. I was a few years behind them, never really a part of the crowd."

"The scandals must have shocked you then?"

"I never could understand how they could have done what they did."

"And Jack Molinas?"

"He was brilliant. He could have made a great success. I never could understand why he turned out that way."

Chapter Twelve

Conclusion:
Misuse of People

It is clear that exploiters, in all aspects of their lives, leave havoc and destruction in their wake. The people I focused on broke laws, cheated, defrauded people and in the process damaged their own lives and the lives of those close to them. These people felt that they had the right to treat others with contempt and deceit. Their lack of concern and scorn for others, coupled with their ability to manipulate people, are the constants in the exploiter profile.

Exploiters cut across diagnostic boundaries. Some can be seen as neurotics, while others border on the psychotic. Exploitation, then, is not so much a diagnostic category as it is a way of thinking and acting in which one aims to extract from others certain advantages and in the process impinges on the rights of others. The goal of exploiters is not to hurt others, but it invariably ends up that way. Exploiters rationalize that what is being done is rightfully theirs to do.

I have pointed out that exploitation of others can take place in a variety of settings and that exploitation can become physical at times. Noteworthy are the cases. The exploiters' delusional thinking resulted in their deaths. Other exploiters steal money, and as I tried to show, a perverse state of mind enabled them to live with this fraudulent behavior and continue their lives as if nothing terrible was happening. Most of us could not explain this to ourselves in a way that would enable us to tolerate the unbearable truth that we are hurting others in the process and breaking the law. The interesting part of the puzzle is that exploiters have this extra sense about themselves and their entitlements that enable them to break any law that stands in their way.

The person who schemes to get ahead creates an interesting dilemma for our society. We look up to people who are able to put their ideas into action and find success in our competitive world. However, in this pursuit there are certain restraints on the exercise of cleverness. The person should not cheat, lie, or hurt others or take unfair advantage of another person's limited capabilities. In all societies, fraud is against the law and results in restitution and punishment. The financial world is always facing conflicts between the need to protect the public from dishonesty and the need not to unduly restrain the enterprising corporation or businessman. To exploit others really means to lie, cheat, deceive, sneak, or defraud. To override proper boundaries between people is not always an issue of criminal activity. This is vividly demonstrated in the film *All About Eve*, in which the title character seeks to advance her career at the expense of a woman she claims to idolize. To deceive and manipulate, to trick with shrewd and clever tactics is surely a basic illness of modern society.

Exploitation involves a number of factors. There needs to be an intention to influence another person by the use of deception and insincerity. Or when it applies to a sport, industry, or organization, exploiters use unfair advantages to corrupt the institution for their own gain. At times there is a secret sense of exhilaration about putting something over on the other person. There is always some idea of tricking or cheating.

Take an instance of a man dating a woman. He wants to get her into, bed but she isn't going for it. He tries to persuade her but runs up against her resistance. So he tells her how wonderful she is, that he feels as if he could be in a long-term relationship with her, and so forth, and at this point she consents to his seduction. However, underneath it all he has no intention of wanting to see her much longer, and when he withdraws from the relationship she is hurt and suffers a loss in self-esteem.

I would call this fellow an exploiter. He resorted to unfair advantage in interpersonal affairs. He lied and deceived to get his way with little regard for the woman's feelings.

In another vein, think of the situation of Marion Jones. She won three gold medals and two bronze medals in the Sydney 2000 Olympics, becoming the first female athlete to win five medals in track and field in one Olympics. Then on January 11, 2008, she was sentenced to six months in prison and ordered to perform eight hundred hours of community service after she pleaded guilty to lying to federal agents about her use of performance-enhancing drugs and her connection to a check fraud case.

The sentencing certainly marked a tragic end to what began as a promising athletic career. Jones broke records in track and field events while in high school and was considered the greatest female athlete of her time. Why would she use steroids to gain an advantage when she could win without them? In addition, she knew it was against the law and then lied about it. She exploited the sport and her fellow athletes. It is difficult to understand her need for such unfair advantages when she was so good to begin with. Jones was in the prime of her career. She must have felt as if she was putting it over on everyone and that by resorting to trickery even while denying in some ways what she was doing, she would be believed as well as inviting compassion. When questioned about her lying, Jones responded by saying that she was a product of an unhappy childhood so that the judge would take pity on her. Jones found it hard to come to grips with how much she tarnished the good name of the sport.

Some exploiters' profiles resemble those of psychopaths. The psychopath is often characterized as essentially "ethically defective." In a civilized society there has always been tension between men of ruthless egotism, the exploiters and predators, and men who have felt strongly about the needs and distresses of others, the men of compassion and righteousness. Can this difference be understood entirely as a product of upbringing and other social influences? Is the difference in moral sensitivity between a St. Francis and a Cesar Borgia, between Lincoln and Napoleon, between a Hitler and a Schweitzer, rooted solely in family setting and environment? Or is there a far larger dimension of the concept of evil?

The aggressive exploiter, e.g., Molinas, gratifies himself at a cost to others. He tramples on their rights, takes without giving. He is a predator. World history is filled with such men and women, for no chapter of humanity is larger than that which tells of how one group has invaded another to gain territory or wealth, women, or slaves. Scores of centuries of such behavior have suggested a view of man as a *natural* aggressor, like other predators among the lower animals. Early man turned from exploiting the animal world to exploiting his fellows. The hunter of animals readily became the hunter of men.

The aggressive exploiter has been a source of extraordinary interest to the layman, the novelist, as well as to psychologists. These individuals lack a vital element of human normality. We may encounter some individuals who are notably self-centered, detached in personal relationships, conspicuously hard or cold with perhaps a touch of the predatory manner without knowing it. We can be moved by their charm, their ability to sell their product, a version of themselves they are able to present as one splendid package of success and vitality. From a distance, they can appear awesome, but when we get involved with them we face a troubling and possibly destructive relationship.

A woman troubled with her inability to maintain friendly affection with her husband begins to see him as a person inherently deficient in emotional makeup who intentionally aims to demean her and weaken her resolve. She must then see her problem as no longer rooted in a failure within herself. A son or daughter who hungers for close intimacy with a parent may experience continual frustration when the latter fails to respond with any of the true substance of a caring attitude. Rather, the parent continually aims to diminish the child's self-worth and use the child as an extension of himself or herself.

It is possible to misconstrue the exploiter as a nonconformist, a free spirit who does things that others might wish to do but are stopped by fear or thoughts of social disapproval or conscience. Until one realizes the extent of the exploiters' ability to wreak havoc, it is a great part of their appeal.

The animal predator is commonly known as one who kills and devours another animal. They employ different means of doing this: they hunt actively or sit and wait for prey to approach within striking distance before attacking. Predators are always working out efficient methods to subdue the prey. Some use poison, which cripples the prey before ingesting it, as the box jellyfish does. In some cases venom, as in rattlesnakes and some spiders, paralyzes the prey before the predator begins ingesting it.

Consider the life of the parasite that lives in or on its host and feeds upon it, eventually leading to the host's death. Some parasites do not kill their hosts instantly. However, they are similar to true predators in that the fate of their prey is quite inevitably death. The wasp lays eggs on or in another species such as a caterpillar. Its larva feeds on the growing host, causing it little harm at first, but soon devouring its internal organs until finally destroying the nervous system, resulting in the prey's death.

Predators exhibit a range of behaviors. Many specialize in hunting only one species of prey. Others, like humans, leopards, and dogs are more opportunistic and will eat almost anything. The specialists are usually well suited to capturing their preferred prey. The prey, in turn, are often equally suited to escape the predator. This is called an evolutionary arms race and tends to keep the population of both species in equilibrium.

Many marriages and relationships imitate this predator-prey connection. The man may dominate the woman, extract money from her, try to seduce her friends, rely on her too much, or treat her as if she is a servant. The woman may fall into this role, and then again she may mature and begin to see what he is trying to do to her. At this point the dynamic in the relationship begins to change. She becomes stronger and stands up to him. He either adjusts to it or moves on to another woman where he tries to repeat the behavior.

These types of relationships have existed for many centuries and still exist in many parts of the world. And then women begin to define their position in life differently. They do not want to assume the position of the prey—they want equal status. The predator then has to change and in many cases give up the need to exploit or manipulate.

A similar dynamic goes on in the animal world. Over time species evolve and change. For example, the fast lion attacks the zebra, and then the fastest zebra is able to escape the lion, so it survives and reproduces, and gradually, faster zebras make up more and more of the population. But the fastest lions are able to catch food and eat, so they survive and reproduce, and gradually, faster lions make up more and more of the population. An important thing to realize is that as both organisms become faster in order to survive, their relationships remain the same: because they are both getting faster, neither gets faster in relation to the other.

But in the human race, the prey is able to learn and give up a previous position of victim. Other animals do not have this ability. However, in much of the world, women are still treated as prey.

Financial predators go through a number of stages. First, they detect the prey, perhaps a trusting investor. Next, they manipulate and misuse information to influence them, and finally they enlist the prey in their scheme. This relationship between predator and prey is mostly beneficial to the predator but sometimes it benefits the prey—remember, some investors with Madoff did draw out substantial amounts of money before the Ponzi scheme collapsed of its own weight.

The study of the exploiter can be seen as a study of evil in one of its basic forms. Compared, moreover, to such impersonal processes as disease and natural catastrophes, the behavior rooted in the aggressive exploiter strain is evil in its most personal form. It is internal, within ourselves, evil known at its source.

The study of the exploiter is in essence an exploration of evil in human relationships because one of the greatest enemies of mankind is a common failure to care about what happens to others. It is in this sense that one may interpret the heartfelt edict that sees the worst of all crimes is not to care about your fellow man.

We may wonder about the inner world of the exploiter. Exploiters may wonder, in an academic sort of way, about the pain they cause others, but they are not really bothered by it.

The hunter or the trapper of animals may imagine the pain or fear of his quarry as perhaps a dim and fleeting image of what he might feel himself, but it has little or no effect on him. In the sadist this image actually gives pleasure; in the compassionate it brings a participating distress.

The difference between regarding another as a self-like-me and as an object to be exploited is a crucial distinction in modern warfare. The image of the foe must be radically changed if the soldier is to kill without internal conflict. Indoctrination of the "gook syndrome" coined in WWII, referring to the Japanese, lowers the value of the enemy to that of an animal or to scum—an alien nonentity. Such mental blindness to the humanity of the individual enemy can be, at times, more difficult to maintain.

A writer who wrote on the relationship between settler and native in the advancement of colonialism in the Third World countries once stated, "The settler paints the native as a sort of quintessence of evil." The process "dehumanizes the native...turns him into an animal...The terms the settler uses when he mentions the native are zoologic terms... When the settler seeks to describe the native...he constantly refers to the bestiary."

This was the pattern that determined the relationship between owner and slave in America. Slaves, according to their owners, had little feeling, little intelligence, and an indifference to the fate of their offspring. They were, in the eyes of the owner, not really human.

In warfare, the need for psychic numbing is a relatively modern development. A person conscripted from a civilian occupation must be brutalized to establish the attitude necessary for killing. He must no longer see the foe as his counterpart: a patriot fighting for what he regards as morally just. An image must be created to symbolize an evil to be exterminated.

Live and let live is no motto for an army. Far better to be too savage, too cruel, too barbarous than to possess too much sentimentality and human empathy. If soldiers are to be good for anything, they must be exactly the opposite of reasoning and thinking individuals. Recruits bring with them common moral notions that must be eliminated in order for their barbaric tendencies to come to life.

Professional soldiers may be differently classed to the extent that their temperament predisposes them for their careers. Soldiers have, through the ages, labeled the enemy as a lesser, nonhuman creature. Recently, Muammar el-Qaddafi called his critics stray dogs. Nazis described the Jews as germs, rats, and leeches. Stalin's murderers called Kulaks (affluent peasant farmers) snakes and vermin. The Tutsis during Rwanda's genocide were referred to as cockroaches and rats, and the Janjaweed of Sudan called the victims of their massacres dogs, donkeys, and monkeys.

Whatever the image, they must cast their victims in a certain light that then enables them to cheat or destroy their victims. Or they must convince themselves that what they are doing isn't so bad—the victims can always get more money or they have too much. There is always something that enables exploiters to justify their actions.

The exploiter—the one we see on Wall Street—deals with his deception almost as if it were impersonal; you don't think about feelings. The emotionally normal criminal may experience qualms of conscience if he breaks the code of his subculture, but rarely toward his victim. The attitude is highly selective; the ruthless Mafia member may have close emotional bonds and loyalties within his professional circle and his family. Similarly, we may assume the same behaviors throughout history with "career" predators: the Norsemen, Mongols, pirates, and the desert tribesmen of Asia who systematically preyed upon the settled farmers.

In the animal world, the hierarchy in which each species preys and lives upon another is elementary biology. A frog devours insects and is in turn devoured by a pelican, and so on. The beak and talons of the hawk and the poisonous fangs of the snake are among the numberless symbols of life as sustained by predatory behavior. In this view, the lion's destruction of a deer, the pirate's seizure of a ship, and the thief's invasion of another's property are all sanctified by the same natural order. Man differs only in that he victimizes his own kind as well as the lower forms, having for ages preyed upon his fellows for their wealth and territory.

Psychologists have seen this behavior as no more than an example of the cultural inheritance of learned behavior. Biologists have stressed that despite man's remarkable learning ability, his animal origins must not be overlooked. To assume that human behavior is entirely free of instinctive factors is to return to the pre-Darwinian view of man as a new being, unrelated to a visibly close ancestry.

Seen in the light of man's continuity with these forms, the exploiter may be regarded as a natural descendent of the predatory animal. Granted that the roots of aggression are deeply embedded, it is equally true and more important that a great turning point in the history of organic life began with the emergence of a new trend: revolt against exploitation and compassion for its victims. The origin of the trend has been traced to the maternal animal and may have been limited, in its earliest phase, to the instinctive response to the needs of offspring. The mammal that enters life in a helpless state needs protection and love to mature. Maternal love is in essence the urge to respond to the needs of another creature.

So it is possible that the maternal instinct is the original source of love. Parental behavior among mammals is mainly confined to the mother, while the paternal role is limited. With humans, that has been the case until very recently. Possibly in the beginning, all feelings of a tender, compassionate, altruistic character are extensions and transformations of the maternal instinct and are directly derived from it. In the end, people don't have to be captains of their own ship. Successful people can become deeply intertwined with one another—learning, sharing, suffering, and mentoring one another. Hopefully, this is the goal of mankind.

Bibliography

Apter, M.J. *Danger: Our Quest for Excitement*. Oxford: Oneworld Publications, 2007.

Bailey, K.G. "The Concept of Phylogenetic Regression." *J. Amer. Acad. Psychoanal.* 6 (1978): 5-35.

Blanke, H. and H.B. Wallis. *The Maltese Falcon*. Directed by John Huston. Los Angeles: Warner Bros., 1941.

Brodie, F. *Richard Nixon: The Shaping of his Character*. New York: W. W. Norton & Company, 1981.

Calef, V. and E.M. Weinshel. "Some Clinical Consequences of Introjection: Gaslighting." *Psychoanal Q.* 50 (1981): 44-66.

Chandler, R. and B. Wilder. *Double Indemnity*. Directed by Billy Wilder. Los Angeles: Paramount Pictures, 1944.

Condon, R. *The Manchurian Candidate*. Directed by John Frankenheimer. Los Angeles: United Artists/M.C. Productions, 1962.

Daley, R. and B. Larson. *Play Misty for Me*. Directed by Clint Eastwood. Los Angeles: Universal Pictures/Malpaso, 1971.

Dawkins, R. *The Selfish Gene*. Oxford: Oxford University Press, 1989.

Deutsch, H. "Some Forms of Emotional Disturbance and their Relationship to Schizophrenia." *Psychoanal. Q.* 11 (1942): 301-321.

Dowd, M. "What's Up, Slut?" *New York Times*, July 14, 2006.

Eastwood, C., E. McGinley, and A. Sabbadini. "Play Misty for Me: The Perversion of Love." *Int. J. Psycho-anal.* 87 (2006): 589-597.

Evans. D. Ari: The Life and Times of Aristotle Onassis. New York: Summit Books, 1986.

Fay, S. *Beyond Greed*. New York: Viking Press, 1982.

Feuer, A. "For Ex-Lobbyist Abramoff, a Post-Prison Multimedia Effort at Redemption." *New York Times,* November 13, 2011.

Fishman, S. "Madoff on Madoff." *New York Magazine,* October 31, 2011.

Freud, S. "Those Wrecked by Success." *Standard Edition* 14 (1916): 316-331.

Friedman, M. Type A Behavior: Its Diagnosis and Treatment. New York, Plenum Press, 1996.

Fusaro, C. and R.M. Miller. *What Went Wrong at Enron.* New York: John Wiley and Sons, 2002.

Gediman, H.K. "Imposture, Inauthenticity and Feeling Fraudulent." *J. Amer. Psychoanal. Assn* 33 (1985): 911-935.

Goldman, W. *Misery.* Directed by Rob Reiner. Los Angeles: Castle Rock/Nelson (1990).

Greenacre, P. "The Impostor." *Psychoanal. Q.* 27 (1958): 359-382.

Hamel, G. *Leading the Revolution.* Boston: Harvard Business Press, 2002.

Hornblow Jr., A. *Gaslight.* Directed by George Cukor. Los Angeles; Metro-Goldwyn-Mayer, 1944.

Ibsen, H. *John Gabriel Borkman.* New York: Farrar Straus and Giroux, 1978.

Isaacs, N. *The Great Molinas.* Bethesda: WID Publishing Group, 1992.

Jackson, D. "Nixon." *Life Magazine,* November 6, 1970.

Jaffe, S.R. and S. Lansing. *Fatal Attraction.* Directed by Adrian Lyne. Los Angeles: Paramount Pictures, 1987.

Kamir, O. The Maintenance of Cultural Myths: the Case of Stalking. Michigan: The Univ. of Michigan Press, 2000.

Kessey, D. Your Legs Must Be Singing Grand Opera': Masculinity, Masochism, and Stephen King's *Misery.*" *Am. Imago* 59 (2002): 53-71.

LaFarge, L. "Transferences of Deception." *JAPA* 43 (1995): 765-792.

Lantos, B. "The Two Genetic Derivations of Aggression with Reference to Sublimation." *Int. J. Psycho-Anal.* 39 (1958): 116-120.

Levin, R. "Infantile Omnipotence and Grandiosity." *Psychoanal. Rev.* 73A (1986): 57-76.

Levine, D.P. "The Corrupt Organization." *Human Relations* 58 (2005): 723-740.

Livingstone, D.S. Less than Human: Why We Demean, Enslave, and Exterminate Others. New York: St. Martin's Press, 2011.

Loewenberg, P.J. "Nixon, Hitler and Power: An Ego Psychological Study." *Psychoanal. Inq.* 6 (1986): 27-48.

Long, S. The Perverse Organization and its Deadly Sins. New York: Karnac Books, 2008.

Maccoby, M. *The Gamesman.* New York: Simon and Schuster, 1977.

Mandel, O. *The Theatre of Don Juan.* Lincoln, Neb.: Univ. of Nebraska Press, 1963.

McLean, B. and P. Elkind. The Smartest Guys in the Room: The Amazing Rise and Scandalous Fall of Enron. New York: **Bethany McLean**

Meloy, J.R. *The Psychopathic Mind.* New York: Jason Aronson, 1988.

Michener. J. *Iberia.* New York: Fawcett Crest Books, 1984.

Miller, M. Plain Speaking. An Oral biography of Harry S. Truman. New York: Tess Press, 2005.

de Molina, T. *Damned for Despair.* Trans. N.G. Round. Oxford: Oxbow Books, 1986.

Moses, R. and R. Moses-Hrushovski. "Reflections on the sense of entitlement." *Psychoanal. St. Child.* 45 (1990): 61-78.

Nixon, R. *SixCrisis.* New York: Doubleday & Company. 1961.

Orr, M. *The Wisdom of Eve.* New York: Dramatists Play Service, Inc., 1994.

Olivier, L. *On Acting.* New York: Simon & Schuster, 1987.

Potter, S. *The Theory and Practice of Gamesmanship.* London: BN Publishing, 2008.

Rangell, L. "Lessons From Watergate. A derivative for psychoanalysis." *Psychoanal. Q.* 45(1) (1975): 37-61.

Rangell, L. *The Mind of Watergate.* New York: W. W. Norton & Co., 1980.

Reich, A. "Pathologic forms of self-esteem regulation." *Psychoanal. St. Child* 15 (1960): 215-232.

Rosen, C. The Wizard of Odds. How Jack Molinas Almost Destroyed the Game of Basketball. New York: Seven Stories Press, 2002.

Ross, N. "The 'As If' Concept." *J. Amer.Psychoanal Assn.* 15 (Feb. 1967): 59-82.

Stein, B.J. License to Steal: The Untold Story of Michael Milken and the Conspiracy to Bilk the Nation. New York: Simon & Schuster, 1992.

Steiner, R. "Some thoughts about tradition and chance arising from an examination of the British Psychoanalytic Societies." *R. of Psycho-Anal.* 12 (1985): 27-71.

Stendahl. *The Red and the Black*. New York: Penguin Classics, 1953.

Stewart, J.B. Den of Thieves. New York: Simon & Schuster. 1991.

Stone, P.H. Heist: Superlobbyist Jack Abramoff, his Republican allies, and the buying of Washington. New York: Farrar, Straus and Giroux, 2006.

Surowiecki, J., (ed). *Best Business Crime Writing of the Year.* New York: Anchor Books, 2002.

Swanson, D. J. "Interview with Bunker Hunt." *The Dallas Morning News*, March 22, 2009.

Morris, E. *Tabloid*. Directed by Errol Morris. New York: IFC. 2010.

Tenzer, A. "Grandiosity and its Discontents." *Contemp. Psychoanal.* 23 (1987): 263-27.

Toffler, B. L. Final Accounting: Ambition Greed and the Fall of Arthur Andersen. New York: Broadway Books, 2003.

Volkan, V.D., N. Itzowitz, and A. Dodd. W. *Richard Nixon: A Psychobiography*. New York: Columbia University Press, 1997.

Weinstein, L. *The Metamorphoses of Don Juan*. Stanford, Calif.: Stanford Univ. Press, 1959.

Welles, O. *The Lady from Shanghai*. Directed by Orson Welles. Los Angeles: Columbia Pictures, 1947.

Wikipedia 1946. "Elmyr De Hory." http://en.wikipedia.org/wiki/Elmyr_de_Hory.

Winter, D.G. *The Power Motive*. New York: The Free Press, 1973.

Wolfe, T. *The Bonfire of the Vanities*. New York: Farrar, Straus and Giroux. 1987.

Zanuck, D.F. *All About Eve*. Directed by Joseph L. Mankiewicz. Los Angeles: 20th Century Fox, 1950.

Dr. Harvey A. Kaplan is a psychotherapist who lives and practices in New York City